Help for Your Shy Dog

Turning Your Terrified Dog into a Terrific Pet

Deborah Wood

Illustrations by Amy Aitken

 Howell Book House
New York

Some of the information in this book should be acted upon by experienced persons only. Furthermore, the book is not intended as a substitute for medical advice of licensed veterinarians. The information provided is for the purposes of education and to give as complete a picture as possible. The reader should regularly consult a veterinarian in matters relating to his or her dog's health, and particularly in regard to any symptoms that may require diagnosis or medical attention.

Howell Book House
An Imprint of IDG Books Worldwide, Inc.
An International Data Group Company
919 E. Hillsdale Boulevard
Foster City, CA 94404

Library of Congress Cataloging-in-Publication Data
Wood, Deborah, 1952–
    Help for your shy dog : turning your terrified dog into a terrific pet / by Deborah Wood ; illustrations by Amy Aitkin.
    p. cm.
    ISBN 0-87605-036-4
    1. Dogs—Behavior.   2. Dogs—Training.   3. Fear in animals.
I. Title.
SF433.W64   1999
636.7'0887—dc21   99-25455
                                                                    CIP

Photo Credits:
  1.4 - Goldie: Kathi Lamm
  2.3 - Weazie: Jerry Vavra Photography
  3.3 - Nellie: Jean Kunkle
  4.3 - Challenge: Barbara Griffin
  5.2 - Tarah: Ellie Wyckoff
  6.2 - Colter: Bob and Lana Lackey
  7.2 - Reno: Deborah Wood
  8.2 - Tess: Jerry Vavra Photography
  9.2 - Briggs: Linda Lindt

  Back cover: Kathi Lamm

Portions of this book first appeared in *Off-Lead* magazine and are reprinted by permission of the Publisher.

10 9 8 7 6 5

To my terrific dog, Goldie. Whatever I've done for you sweet dog, you've returned the favor to me a thousand times.

Acknowledgments

This book was the idea of Lorenz "Don" Arner, publisher of *Off-Lead* magazine. Without Don's guidance and encouragement, this book would never have been written.

My brother, Frank E. Wood, was a brilliant creative inspiration. It's great to have such a talented relative—who is also my friend.

Many dedicated people who care greatly about their dogs have given me a lot of information and insights. Special thanks go to the people whose wonderful dogs appear on the pages of this book. Shannon Chenault, Peggy Gainer, Barbara Griffin, Jean Kunkle, Bob and Lana Lackey, Wanda Packard, Chris and Jim Primmer, and Claudia VanGee taught me a great deal about what works in helping fearful dogs. They also are living examples of kindness and understanding toward the dogs they love.

Many other people gave me dog advice and technical information that helped enormously. They include Robert Anderson, D.V.M.; Leah Atwood; Nancy Ballerstedt; Cynthia Bradley; Tommie Brunick; David and Donna Elizares; Chris Hanna, of *Front and Finish* magazine; Kim James; Judge Michael H. Marcus; Mary O'Neil; Charm Preston; and Ellie Wyckoff. Their wisdom is included in these pages.

Thanks also to all of my classmates in my training classes over the years. We all learn from each other. Thanks to my friends at RiverPlace Book Merchants, Betty Pakenen and Howard Lucas, who read early

drafts of the book and gave me great constructive criticism—and convinced me I could write a book.

I wrote this book while I struggled with chronic fatigue syndrome.
Thanks to Professor Chen Hui Xian, Dr. David Eisen, Linda Gaeth,
Dr. Donald Girard, Susan Murphy, and Dr. Arlette Sieckman, my team
of Western and alternative medical practitioners, for helping me be well
enough to write.

Contents

Foreword

In 1996, Deborah Wood wrote an article she called "From Terrified to Terrific: Ten Lessons for Training and Socializing Timid Dogs." She submitted the article to *Off-Lead*, the international dog trainer's magazine. As the magazine's editor and publisher, I was extraordinarily pleased to read an article that brought new ideas to the world of dog training and behavior. I called Deborah on the phone, told her we wanted to publish her article, and said, "Write a book!" The result, this book, is the most important contribution to enjoyable dog companionship since the "clicker."

The world is full of fearful dogs and owners who haven't the foggiest notion how to change their behavior. Certainly many dog trainers and behaviorists are stumped. In the past, dogs who couldn't be rehabilitated by "current techniques" simply disappeared, and life went on. Most professional counseling amounted to: "Don't waste your time and money on this dog. Get one that has his head on straight."

This book can change all that for you. It outlines a program that will invalidate previous approaches; anyone who follows it is practically guaranteed success. Deborah's book expertly blends her professional background working with emotionally damaged people with her canine experience to present an understanding of the parallels between dog and human behavior. She has successfully simplified the very complex variables and clarified many misconceptions and presented solutions in a way we all can apply successfully.

Some dog owners have neither the time nor the patience to undertake the task. But for those who love their fearful dogs and have these virtues, this book makes the path as clear as it is possible to make it.

They will be listening to a woman who has practiced, with great success, everything she preaches.

It's nice to know my encouragement resulted in a book that will improve the quality of life of so many dogs and their human companions. For many dogs, it will mean their last chance at life. Thank you, Deborah Wood.

—Lorenz "Don" Arner
Publisher and Editor
Off-Lead Magazine

Introduction

L iving with a fearful dog can be a daily sorrow. Watching him pull back in fright from a friendly hand is heart-wrenching. Seeing him shake violently in fear instead of exploring the scents and sights of a walk is inexpressibly sad. If your dog is a fear-biter, you know he's a likely candidate for euthanasia. Your shy dog may be so consumed by his insecurities that he can't express his love for you in the free and giving way that is the essence of the human-dog connection. Your dog is trapped in his own fear just as surely as if he were confined to a stark and sterile cage 24 hours a day.

Your goals may be modest: You just want your dog to stop submissively urinating all over your shoes. You want to be able to take your pet for a walk without him shaking violently in fear. You'd like your dog to be willing to be petted by a friend. You wish he'd wag his tail at another dog instead of cowering in terror. You hope your dog will learn to play. You'd like the sad expression in his eyes to be replaced with the shining look of happiness typical of a well-adjusted dog. You want to stop feeling that you have to explain to everyone who sees your dog that you're really a nice person and haven't beaten him; it's honestly not your fault that he's cringing and shivering with fear.

Maybe your dog's shyness isn't severe. Perhaps he just doesn't have the confidence to relax and enjoy life as a dog. You'd just like to increase his sense of security and playfulness.

On the bad days, it's easy to believe the people who shake their heads and tell you that your dog is ruined because of the treatment he once received or because of his basic temperament. Don't believe them! With love and the right guidance, almost any dog can transform from fearful to faithful, from terrified to terrific.

Your dog's life doesn't have to be defined by his fears. This book will provide you with specific, practical solutions to the problems faced by your timid dog. Following the methods outlined in this book, your dog will turn into a great companion animal.

Most of the advice in this book won't take an extra minute of your time. You'll learn how to use your voice and body to allay his fears. You'll find out how to make your walks with your dog opportunities for him to heal (as well as "heel"). You'll find out how to pick a trainer who can make working with your dog a pleasure. You'll also learn about activities to do with your dog that will be fun for both of you.

In addition to providing practical advice for reshaping your dog's behavior, this book tells the stories of nine fearful dogs. Each of these dogs has a unique story. Each mastered some special accomplishments. Some of the dogs profiled went from fearful, cringing dogs to become "super dogs" boasting extraordinary accomplishments in obedience and agility competitions. All the dogs in the book went on to become first-class family pets. These dogs are testimonials that, with love and some work, your dog can exceed your highest expectations.

You and your dog are about to undertake a magical journey. You'll be a witness to your dog's courage as he struggles with his fears and learns to trust. Eventually, you'll share the great joy of the bond of loyalty and love that can develop between the two of you when you help your pet overcome his problems. Your shy dog can become the best pet you've ever had.

You hope your dog will learn to play.

Would I recommend that someone deliberately go out and get a frightened dog? Probably not. But if a fearful dog has selected you, don't back off from the challenge. Years of happy companionship can lie ahead.

Now, let's get to the task of helping your dog become the pet you've always dreamed of!

Chapter One

Understanding: The First Step on the Road to Recovery

Many timid and fearful dogs weren't given proper socialization.

Your shy dog isn't alone: Shyness ranks behind only aggression as the most common behavioral problem in dogs. Understanding the causes of this pervasive problem, however, can help you provide the guidance that your dog needs to overcome her fear.

THE FOUR CAUSES OF FEARFUL PERSONALITIES

Why isn't your dog like your neighbor's bold, outgoing dog? Dogs develop fearful behavior for the same reasons that humans become shy and withdrawn: physical infirmity, lack of proper socialization, abuse, and genetic programming. Some fearful dogs have a combination of these problems.

Physical Infirmity

Physical pain can make a dog act frightened or shy. For example, a dog who can't see well may become a biter out of fear, since she can't see an approaching person's hand until the hand is right in her face. A dog with back pain or hip dysplasia also may shrink away from human contact if even a gentle touch aggravates her condition. Pain also might cause a dog to quiver, making her look as if she's shaking nervously.

Before assuming your dog is shy, have her checked thoroughly by a veterinarian. It's possible your dog has a physical ailment that can be corrected, and the treatment might transform her into an outgoing, friendly pet.

Of course, you may find that your dog's fearful attitude is caused by a physical ailment that your veterinarian can't treat successfully. Many of the methods outlined in this book for boosting a fearful dog's confidence also help a dog overcome the shyness created by an injury or illness. You may both live a happier life after following these suggestions.

Lack of Socialization

Your dog's problems may have started in her childhood if she wasn't given proper socialization. Just as human children who aren't given time, attention and learning opportunities often develop poor coping skills, puppies who don't have an enriched environment can have a difficult time adjusting to new situations throughout their lives.

Where do you find poorly socialized dogs? Here are some examples:

• **Animal shelters.** The following situation is typical of a dog who ends up at a local animal shelter. A well-meaning husband and wife purchase a dog because they always admired the intelligence of the active, working breed. The man and woman both work full-time. After the puppy destroys the sofa, she's kept confined to the windowless laundry room for 12 hours a day. Despite their best intentions, the man and woman are tired after their long, hard days of work, and they give the dog little attention and less exercise. After 18 months, the husband and wife decide that they have the only neurotic idiot ever whelped of the intelligent breed, and they take the dog to the local animal shelter. The dog is overwhelmed at the shelter because she hasn't seen another dog since she was 8 weeks old. She shivers in fear.

An amazing number of people buy dogs with no concept of the care and attention dogs require. These people seem to think that raising a dog takes about the same amount of time as caring for a mellow cat—or perhaps a stuffed animal. Many of their pets end up in animal shelters throughout the nation.

• **Pet shops.** Wholesale breeders breed purebred or small mixed-breed dogs for sale to pet shops. The conditions at these "puppy mills" are designed to cost the breeders as little as possible and to produce as many puppies as possible. Often, conditions are unspeakably inhumane, with filthy, overcrowded pens and undernourished dogs. Females may be bred every time they come into season, which makes for a dangerous practice. Puppies, who aren't socialized at all, are shipped to pet stores, where conditions are not enormously better.

Pet store puppies usually live in tiny cages and are subjected to the stress of massive numbers of people poking and prodding at them. It should come as no surprise that pet store puppies often suffer from a variety of problems, including shyness.

If you've already purchased a dog at a pet shop and are doing your earnest best to turn her into a happy, well-adjusted pet, read on! After all, when your dog pulled your heart strings at the pet shop, you didn't know the commercial puppy industry is an ugly business. This book should help you give the dog the break she needs.

- **Show dog kennels.** A show dog breeder can be the best place to purchase a new puppy. Most care enormously about their chosen breeds, including the health and temperament of the parents and their offspring. Owners of some of the dogs who are profiled in this book are dog show exhibitors, and they're among the kindest, most caring dog owners you'll find anywhere.

But you'll find others in the dog show world as well. Although they represent a minority, some show dog breeders view their dogs as a commodity and pay attention only to those dogs who have the looks and personality to be top winners. The busy breeder may have little time to socialize and play with the dogs who aren't the current hot prospects for showing and breeding. Although kept clean and well fed, the forgotten dog in a show dog kennel can develop into a very shy dog.

Abuse

Humans have invented countless ways to torture innocent animals. Whether a one-time incident or abuse over the course of months or years, traumatic experiences are powerful destroyers of the human-animal bond.

It's no wonder that an abused dog grows into a fearful, confused adult. She has no road map to know what actions will bring pain, so she crouches in a corner and tries to do nothing—or she may try to bite, figuring the best defense is a good offense.

For most of us, dog abuse is defined by the horror stories we see on the local evening news. The reality is that most abuse is more ordinary than the stories that capture the headlines. Although adults may perpetrate the most hideous crimes against dogs, children are the most frequent abusers. Children younger than about age 6 can't entirely distinguish between a living dog and a toy. Likewise, older children can act carelessly or might not have been taught the proper way to treat a dog. In any event, small children might chase and scream at dogs, hit them with sticks, and use them as footballs. Rough-and-tumble roughhousing that might be fine for a large dog can break the bones of a small dog—and the person who abuses a dog might be an angelic-looking 10-year-old.

Genetics

A dog's genetic programming is a crucial determinant of her response to life's situations. Most scientific research indicates that about half of an animal's (or a human's) personality is defined by her environment; the other half is determined by her genetic makeup. For instance, your fearful dog may not have experienced a bad day in her life. She may be the picture of health, live in a loving and varied environment, and have never faced a traumatic situation—yet she might still be extremely fearful. Just as some humans are born shy, some dogs are born with fearful temperaments.

A dog's assimilation of her experiences is largely determined by her genetic wiring. For example, four dogs that have been left alone for months in a backyard and given virtually no human attention may have four entirely different reactions when they are placed in loving homes: One may bond instantly with her new owners, apparently happy and grateful to be rescued; another may be difficult to control because she's insatiably curious about her new surroundings; the third may become uncontrollably aggressive; and the final one may shake in fear at the change in her surroundings. The differences in these dogs' reactions are probably genetically determined.

The differences in these dogs' reactions are probably genetically determined.

All species (including humans) have individuals who display shy, risk-averse behavior. Studies indicate that about 15 to 20 percent of the population of any species of higher animals will be born prone to introversion and fear.

WARRIORS AND WORRIERS

A compelling argument can be made that some dogs are genetically wired for caution as part of the species' survival mechanisms. A pack of wild dogs needs leaders who will explore new territory and hunt new things. But the pack also needs members who hold back to make sure the leader isn't leading them off the edge of a cliff! Introverted, cautious behavior is just as important in the mix of personalities in the pack as bold, friendly behavior. Every pack needs its warriors and its worriers, which means that your shy dog isn't inherently a worse animal; she's just on one end of the spectrum of animal behavior.

Although shy individuals exist in every dog breed, shyness is more common in some breeds than others. It's more common to see a shy Shetland Sheepdog than a reticent Rottweiler. Likewise, petrified Papillons are more common than bashful Basenjis.

Humans have selectively bred dogs for traits that can result in shy or fearful behavior. As one Shetland Sheepdog owner put it, "The desired personality of the breed is independent and a bit reserved. Imagine how important this would be on a hillside guarding sheep with the sheep herder in a remote area of the Shetland Islands." In fact, the American Kennel Club breed standards for several herding dogs make references to these breeds' distrust of strangers—an obvious asset for dogs who tend flocks. Terms used in the herding breed standards include: "suspicious of strangers," "reserved with strangers," "observant and vigilant with strangers," "sensibly suspicious," and "watchful and reserved." That reserved and suspicious quality makes the dog a better tender of the flock. You don't want a working sheep-tending dog to see a pack of hungry wolves and decide to go over and make some new pals. In that context, a suspicious nature is a valuable asset. Taken a bit further, it's a small step for a dog who's been bred to be suspicious and reserved to develop shyness and even fear of strangers.

Just as we've bred herding dogs who have a tendency to be reserved with strangers, we've bred other types of dogs to be very submissive to us. We want our toy breeds to sit on our laps and follow us from room to room as constant companions. A submissive, affectionate nature makes a great companion dog, but sometimes the same genes that create a submissive companion can also create an overly submissive, insecure dog. Similarly, we want hunting dogs who will put aside their hunting drive and retrieve game for us, but the same genetic tendencies that make a loyal game dog can also make an overly dependent, nervous dog.

Although shyness is more common in some breeds than others, no breed is exempt. In fact, breeds that have been developed for protection or that are otherwise naturally more aggressive can pose special difficulties, since these dogs are the most likely to become fear-biters.

The most difficult dogs to help are those who have both a strong genetic tendency toward fear and also have had a history of abuse or neglect. These dogs take special patience, and their owners face the longest, most trying road to travel in leading their pets to a happy, people-oriented life.

YOUR DOG CAN GET BETTER

You may never know the cause of your dog's fearfulness. No matter what triggered your dog's shy behavior patterns, though, it's time to give her the opportunity to change.

If you've read much of the recent dog behavior literature, you may have read that fearful dogs will never change their behavior. I remember my anger as I read a column in a nationally distributed dog magazine. The columnist, who was writing about her experiences with a former dog, explained that she'd brought the dog home at 12 weeks of age and that the damage had already been done because dogs' temperaments are determined in the early weeks of puppyhood. She wrote that in some ways it was a relief when the dog died 10 years later. This writer bought into the belief that fearful dogs can't ever get better. The truth, however, is that they can.

At the time I read that column, I was well on my way to transforming my own dog from a fearful, shivering, sad-eyed dog to a happy, loving bundle of energy. I knew from my experience with my dog not to trust the words of the columnist.

I had another reason for not trusting that advice. For 15 years, I ran housing and social-service programs for low-income and homeless people. Many of those people had been abandoned, abused and beaten when they were children. Many had lived on the streets for decades, unloved and unwanted. Yet, I saw those people change.

People can—and do—reintegrate into the larger society every day. I've seen people who were literally tortured as children learn to lead happy and dignified adult lives. I've seen men and women who lived on the streets for decades come inside and become thoughtful and supportive neighbors.

It's outdated thinking to assume that people with bad childhoods never overcome their experiences. Similarly, it's outdated thinking to assume that a dog with less-than-perfect socialization can't overcome that deficit with the right kind of care and attention.

Of course, there's also the opposite side of the spectrum. Some people believe that, with just a little love, any dog will blossom into a happy, affectionate pet. If only it were that simple!

Caring for a fearful dog is analogous to adopting an older child with multiple problems. Back in the 1950s, families adopted such children with the assumption that a stable family environment would automatically create trust and happiness in the adopted child. Adoptive parents were shocked and heartbroken when these children frequently developed serious emotional problems. We've learned a lot since then: We know that children with special problems can be successfully adopted by a loving family, but it takes a combination of counseling, structure, patience and a lot of love to make it succeed. Similarly, someone who has a fearful dog needs to do more than just love the creature. The steps outlined in this book will provide the tools to address your dog's multiple problems.

How Long Does This Recovery Take?

How confident your dog can become and the time period it takes to achieve acceptable behavior depends on four variables:

- Your commitment of time and willingness to follow proven techniques
- Your dog's socialization as a puppy
- Abuse or neglect your dog has experienced
- Your dog's genetic predisposition to shyness

Some lucky people get apparently fearful dogs who quickly transform into happy, trusting, easy-going pets. In these cases, the dogs were probably born with extroverted tendencies. In all likelihood, such dogs also had good early socialization, and the fearful behavior was triggered by an episode of abuse or neglect. Once such temperamentally sound dogs figure out the abuse is over, they become the outgoing dogs they were destined to be. Although it's great when this happens, such cases unfortunately are relatively rare.

One owner of a shy dog who has succeeded in many competitive endeavors explained to me that a dog's basic personality doesn't change. However, a fearful dog can learn to compensate for her shyness. The more training she receives and the more situations she experiences, the better she compensates. Your goal with your dog will be to help with the compensation process.

As your dog learns to compensate for her fearfulness, she gains control of her flight or fight response. Over time, the dog learns to accept or ignore things that used to terrify her. Her behavior toward fearful stimuli changes, and she feels safe in a wider range of situations. She learns to relax and even play in conditions that once would have had her running for cover.

For dogs with innate shyness, the process is never over. However, after interviewing many people who have transformed fearful dogs into dogs who perform joyfully in high-stress situations, I've identified some basic benchmarks. If you work diligently with the dog, you can see progress from the beginning. Noticeable changes in behavior usually begin to occur after you've worked with the dog about six months. After about a year and a half, the dog presents a very different demeanor to people who meet the dog for the first time. After about three years, the dog's behavior problems are usually subtle—and are often not visible to people who aren't carefully looking for signs of shyness. These timelines vary, but overcoming fearfulness is usually not a short-term proposition. Fortunately, though, it is a very rewarding one.

Fearful dogs continue to make progress throughout the course of their lives, as long as they have opportunities to do so. Given new situations to conquer, your dog will continue to grow and improve throughout her long life.

No matter what your dog's background or temperament, it's never too late to help her get better!

Goldie: My Dog's Story

Goldie has taught me the magical power of healing and renewal.

Since I was a child, I had wanted a Papillon. Papillons are a tiny, highly intelligent breed named for the enormous ears that frame their faces like butterfly wings (*Papillon* is the French word for *butterfly*). I contacted people who had exhibited their dogs at a local dog show and went to see Goldie, a 2-year-old who was for sale.

When Goldie was brought out from her crate, she looked at me with liquid, timid eyes. She shook nervously. After several minutes, I was finally able to persuade her to take a bit of the liver I held in my hand.

Then it happened: Something between us connected. Soon Goldie was lying on her back, contentedly nibbling my fingers as I gently rubbed her tummy. Goldie made it clear she'd selected me.

Homecoming

The Papillon I had always envisioned owning had the outgoing, merry disposition typical of the breed. Instead, the Papillon I took home was a terrified creature. She didn't know her own name. She didn't know how to walk up and down stairs. She was afraid of the sky. She fled from small birds. She shook violently whenever we left my condominium, even to go into the building's quiet courtyard. It took her six months before she wagged her tail.

Her physical appearance indicated her failure to thrive. Her coat, which should have been long and silky, was sparse and harsh. She was underweight and showed little interest in food.

I was a knowledgeable dog owner. I knew Goldie would be more work than other dogs, and I thought I knew what I was getting into.

I didn't have a clue.

The Right Start

When I realized that I was in over my head, I took Goldie to a local dog obedience school. It made her worse.

I looked for help in dog training books and dog magazines, but these publications mentioned little about fearful dogs. The most common advice was to be sure never to bring home a timid dog, since fearful dogs make poor pets.

After eight months of owning Goldie, I'd seen her improve only marginally. She still shook violently in any new situation, would seldom play with her toys and would relate to no one other than me.

Fortunately, I found the tutelage of some very experienced dog trainers who helped me discover the Goldie who was locked inside the fearful dog I'd brought home. Five years after Goldie came into my life, she's now a happy, healthy 7-year-old. She has earned her Companion Dog Obedience title and her AKC Canine Good Citizen certificate. She loves to go for walks and is a world-class pigeon chaser. Her coat is soft, glossy and luxurious. I even receive constant compliments on her sweet personality and good manners.

Facing Fears

Yet Goldie still bears some traces of the frightened dog she once was. She no longer cowers from strangers, but she looks at them with clear skepticism. Some people describe her as aloof. I just smile—I can live with an aloof dog who takes a few minutes to get her bearings in unfamiliar surroundings. That's a lot different than a fearful animal experiencing constant, overwhelming panic.

Watching Goldie courageously face her fears and choose to trust others has been an extraordinary experience. She has become so bonded to me in this process that our relationship is impossible to describe: It feels as if we're inside each other's minds. Goldie has taught me the magical power of healing and renewal, and I wouldn't have missed the joys of sharing my life with Goldie for all the world.

Chapter Two

Socialization: Teaching Your Dog to Cope

Your dog will give you signs when he's nervous.

Conventional wisdom holds that socialization is key to rehabilitating a fearful dog. That conventional wisdom is right, but those conventionally wise people hardly ever give any details. How far should you push your dog before it's too much? How do you know when you're expanding your dog's ability to cope and when you're adding to his fear?

Ask your dog.

Your dog will give you signs when he's nervous. He'll let you know whether he's just experiencing a little apprehension, or whether he's in a state of panic. You expect your dog to listen to you and to understand a wide range of your words and routines. If you reciprocate and learn to understand what your dog is telling you, his rehabilitation will go much faster.

LEARNING TO READ YOUR DOG

Your dog will tell you what level of activity he can handle. Use this as a starting point for all kinds of communication the two of you will share.

Watch for These Signs

Signs of fear generally become apparent in this progressive order.

1. Yawning. Most people believe that a dog yawns as a sign of relaxation, since we as people yawn when we're sleepy or relaxed. However, quick yawns are a sign of nervousness in dogs and may be your first indication that your dog is feeling anxiety. If the dog's body language is otherwise positive, a yawn indicates fairly minor nervousness, but you still should realize that your dog is experiencing some level of stress. Lengthy exposure to situations that cause your dog to yawn nervously will tire him and may cause his stress levels to escalate.

Of course, dogs also yawn when they're sleepy. If your dog is snug in his bed about to go to sleep, his long, slow yawn is obviously not a sign of anxiety. Nervous yawns are quicker yawns, and your dog's body will be tense, not relaxed.

2. Pinning back his ears. A happy, confident dog will stick his ears forward. A dog with his ears pinned backward, on the other hand, is feeling tension. If his body posture is otherwise confident, the dog isn't feeling extreme stress, but he's warning you that he's apprehensive.

3. Tucking his tail between his legs. A classic sign of fear and submission is tucking the tail between legs. In this case, the dog is warning you that he's feeling uncomfortably apprehensive.

4. Shaking. Shaking is a sign of a high level of stress. Although it's most common in small dogs, fearful dogs of all sizes will respond to stressful situations by shaking violently.

5. Crouching. A dog who puts his head low to the ground, arches his back and tucks his tail between his legs is expressing a very high level of stress and submission.

If a crouched posture, with ears back and the tail between the legs, is accompanied by growling, watch out! This is the classic fear-biting stance. Your dog is in a panic and isn't capable of listening to you. Immediately remove the dog from the situation and try to eliminate the source of his fear. If you don't, major trouble could erupt at any instant.

6. Urinating submissively. Nervous dogs will urinate to show their submission to the dominant dogs in the pack. It's basically the dog equivalent of the person who says, "I was so nervous I thought I'd wet my pants."

7. Defecating. As if submissive urination isn't unpleasant enough, fearful dogs will often defecate in situations in which they feel intimidated. Of course, dogs most often feel intimidated in very public places—no one said that owning a nervous dog was going to be glamorous!

The Eyes Have It

More than any other sign, watch your dog's eyes. Undoubtedly, you already recognize the look of fear in his eyes, and you've seen his expression when he's panicked. Watch for changes in your dog's expression.

Over time, you'll see his look of fear ebb away. Often, the habits of fear will last longer than the fear itself, and your dog's eyes can relay this information to you. For example, your dog may shake violently for a long time after he's fairly desensitized to the fear of going to new places. The look in your dog's eyes will change long before his body is willing to give up the habit of shaking when he goes to an unfamiliar location.

Observe your dog carefully and learn to recognize the information that he's conveying, to you. After all, if you understand the signs of nervousness, apprehension and fear, you can better help your dog overcome his problems.

GETTING OUT IN THE REAL WORLD

Introducing your fearful dog to new situations is a gradual process. You'll have to balance his need to be exposed to a wide variety of circumstances with his need to keep his anxiety about new situations at a controllable level.

Stretching Your Dog's Comfort Zone

Your dog is never going to conquer his fear sitting in your house or backyard. He needs the experience of seeing new people, exploring new places and reacting to a variety of situations.

It can be embarrassing to take your fearful dog out in public at first. He may decide to do doggie submissive behavior, such as urination or defecation, at the most humiliating moments. He may shake and shiver so much that people will look at you as if you surely must have beaten the poor dog.

When I first started to take Goldie places, I wanted to wear a T-shirt proclaiming that my dog was under new management. When I bumped into a friend of mine on the street, she didn't exactly admire my beautiful dog; instead, she laughed and said, "Gees, you put in a quarter and she vibrates."

Even if it causes you some embarrassment, though, you must take your dog outside his zone of comfort to show him that he's got the ability to cope. When you do so, you need to display the happy, confident tone of voice and body language to reaffirm that he has nothing to fear.

A fearful dog is like the child who decides he or she doesn't have the ability to learn something. If little Susie said, "I can't take math class; it's too hard for me," you wouldn't respond to the problem by allowing Susie to go through life without math. Instead, you'd ensure that she took a math class at the proper level for her skill and ability. When Susie succeeds, her self-confidence improves, and she'll approach future challenges with more assurance.

The same will be true for your dog. Once he starts overcoming his fears, he'll learn to face future challenges with more confidence.

On the other hand, don't give your dog more of a challenge than he's ready to face, or it will compound his fear. Let's continue with the example of the child who's afraid of taking math classes. If Susie is put into a math class at a level at which she can succeed, her self-esteem greatly increases. However, if Susie is placed in a calculus class, her failure to work at that level will reinforce her belief that she can't do math. Start your dog out slowly, and work up to more-challenging situations.

A woman with a shy dog recently said to me, "When I started out with my dog, I tried to put him in the middle of every situation I could. I finally figured out I was wrong. We should have started out on the sidelines and worked up to the middle." As you introduce your dog to situations, watch his reaction. Does he calm down after a few minutes, or does his fear escalate? If he doesn't begin to show fewer signs of fear within about 10 minutes, the situation you've put him in is too demanding for him at this point in his development.

Watch to see if your dog has a time limit in a setting. He may be relatively calm for 15 minutes or an hour, but suddenly he'll let you know he's had enough. Respect his limitations. As you follow the program set out in this book, he'll build up his confidence and become comfortable in an ever-widening set of situations.

Protecting Your Dog

It's absolutely imperative during these early sessions that your dog suffers no bad experiences. After all, he isn't going to get over his fear if he's attacked by a vicious dog on his first outing beyond his yard. He's not going to learn to relax with strangers if a 2-year-old child is allowed to pull his ears and poke at his eyes. It's your responsibility to protect your dog from harm.

When you start out, it's best not to let strangers pet your dog. When your dog is ready to interact with strangers, allow only one person at a time to pet him. Even with a confident, outgoing dog, one person at a time should always be the limit. It doesn't take long for a dog to feel stressed and frightened by several people circling and grabbing at him. At the point your dog is ready to be approached by strangers, make it clear that you won't tolerate a mob scene.

Your first goal is to help your dog learn that simple walks aren't going to harm him. Over time, you'll work up from short, uneventful walks in your neighborhood to excursions to busy places where he'll be petted by people of all ages. Keep your first steps modest, though; you'll tackle the longer walks later.

HELPING YOUR DOG COPE

1. Introduce the collar and leash. Part of your fearful dog's transformation will hinge on walks with you. To go on these walks, he must be under safe control with a collar and a leash. Get him a sturdy buckle collar that fits properly, and let him wear it around the house until he's perfectly comfortable. Then put a leash on him for a few minutes at a time, and follow him around the house and yard. When he's comfortable walking around with you on the other end of the leash, say "Let's go," and gently lead the way around your yard. It's important for him to be compliant on the leash before you head out into the real world.

2. Go for neighborhood walks. At least twice a day, take your dog on a short walk in your neighborhood. Keep within a block or two of your house. Don't let other people pet him, and don't let him socialize with other dogs. Always keep your dog on the leash: A fearful dog's reaction to a startling sound or event could well send him fleeing from the noise—straight into traffic.

Does he go with you on these walks in a relaxed, confident manner? If so, lucky you! He's ready for the next step: walks in quiet places outside your neighborhood.

For many fearful dogs, though, a simple neighborhood walk will be an overwhelming experience. If this level of activity frightens your dog, continue doing this exercise every day. As long as he's near his home and in no danger, there's no less stressful way to introduce him to the real world.

Keep taking him on these short walks until his signs of fearfulness have diminished. While you walk, talk to your dog in a happy, confident voice. If you have a small dog, remember to make him walk. He won't gain confidence if you carry him everywhere!

If you've just acquired a nervous dog, stay at this level of activity until you're sure the dog has adjusted to his new home. Often, a fearful dog will seem reasonably calm the first several days you take him out, only to exhibit extreme fearful behavior on his outings after a week or two. Once a fearful dog begins to relax and feel comfortable in his new home, the contrast between his feelings of comfort inside your home with the uncertainty of the street can be disconcerting. A nervous dog—particularly one who has been left alone for long hours at a time in a previous home—may actually seem to grow more fearful over the first few weeks with you. Don't give up! Keep walking him.

While you walk, talk to your dog in a happy, confident voice.

If you don't persist with this step, you're condemning your dog to a life within the narrow confines of your home. Zoo animals are given more space. Patiently, lovingly, cheerfully take your dog out day after day. Eventually, you'll be rewarded. A day will come when the dog actually enjoys his walk. He'll begin to display curiosity about what he sees, and he'll look forward to going out with you.

Keep walks short at first—no more than 10 minutes at a time. Also allow your dog time to rest afterward. It takes a lot of his energy to deal with his fear. Give him a tidbit when he's done with his walk, and tell him how proud you are of how hard he's trying.

How do you know if he's ready to graduate from walks in the neighborhood to walks outside the neighborhood? Let him tell you.

If he doesn't regularly display any of the signs of fearfulness, he's definitely ready to go on to the next step. If he shows his anxiety by yawning occasionally, don't be too concerned. Similarly, pinned-back ears only indicate mild apprehension. Talk cheerfully to him (especially when he's indicating a little nervousness with the yawning and the ear movements) and make sure outings aren't so long as to be an ordeal. With these cautions in mind, he's ready to go on beyond your immediate neighborhood.

If your dog tucks his tail between his legs, he's still feeling pretty nervous. Go ahead and try a few walks in quiet places outside your immediate neighborhood. Watch your dog carefully: If he seems overwhelmed and panicked, go back to just walking him in the neighborhood for a while.

If he's shaking violently, crouching, defecating or urinating just from the pressure of walking in the neighborhood, don't overwhelm him with a constant barrage of other experiences. Let him get used to your neighborhood walks, and keep your activities at this level until his signs of fearfulness begin to subside. After he's conquered his worst symptoms, he's ready to try something new.

What should you do if your neighborhood isn't a safe place to walk your dog? Perhaps roving, aggressive dogs in your neighborhood make a walk for your dog a dangerous activity. If your neighborhood isn't a safe place to walk your dog, don't risk it. However, don't give up on introducing your dog to the real world. Just walk him someplace that is safe—a park or an "adopted" safe neighborhood—but expect it to take longer for him to feel comfortable than if you started in your own neighborhood.

3. Take walks in quiet places outside the neighborhood.
Now that your dog has learned to accept walks in his own neighborhood, it's time to graduate to the next level. Take the dog to a safe
place away from your home. Make it a park, a school yard when classes
aren't in session, a safe neighborhood or some other quiet place.
Again, keep him on a leash, but help him explore the sights and
sounds of the environment. Don't allow people to come up and pet
him, though: This walk is just for the two of you.

Odds are good that your dog will be nervous in the new environment. He may show all the same signs of fear that he first showed
during your neighborhood walks. Even if the neighborhood walks
didn't worry him much, going outside the space that smells like home
can trigger fear. If your dog is nervous in the new environment, keep
returning to the same place until he learns to enjoy (or at least
tolerate) his walks there.

Once he's comfortable at the new location, find other quiet loca-
tions to walk your dog. Look for the kind of spots your dog particularly
likes. Most nervous dogs like open spaces best, so look for fields for
your dog to play in. Make sure you spend some time in the areas your
dog is most comfortable, but also expose him to areas that stretch his
comfort zone a little.

Keep returning to each new location until he relaxes. Over time,
he'll look forward to his walks in a new location. He'll eventually even
be curious about new surroundings.

You've accomplished a lot at this point! Your dog is no longer a
prisoner in his own home and yard. He has learned to enjoy, or at least
accept, a variety of places. And he has begun the process of bonding
with you and trusting you.

RIDING IN THE CAR

Many nervous dogs have trouble riding in the car. They may shake
violently and exhibit general terror at the whole concept of hurtling
through space in a machine. Often, nervous dogs get car sick. If your
dog is going to enjoy exploring new places and new neighborhoods,
however, you may need to desensitize him to the experience of riding
in a car.

Basic Car Safety

Before tackling your dog's special problems in the car, it's important to consider basic car safety. People who would never consider riding without their seat belts all too often leave their dogs loose in their cars.

Use the following good-sense safety tips on all trips with your dog:

1. Use a crate. All dogs should ride in a crate. A loose dog can distract the driver, is in grave danger in case of an accident, and is likely to jump out the window when the car is in motion. A plastic crate is sturdiest; a wire crate provides a little less protection in case of an accident, but this type allows you to see the dog and the dog to see the scenery.

2. At the very least, restrain your dog. If you don't want to use a crate, use a doggie seatbelt. This devise consists of a harness with a short leash that attaches to the car seatbelt. It doesn't offer as much protection as a crate, but it will keep your dog confined.

3. Keep the windows closed. If you insist on riding with your dog loose in the car, keep all the windows closed. Never let a dog stick his head out the window; not only might he be tempted to jump out of the car, but he's also very likely to develop ear infections or get foreign objects in his eyes. This practice is unhealthy for the dog and a source of potentially huge vet bills for you.

4. Don't travel in pickup trucks. Never, ever let a dog ride loose in the back of a pickup truck! Many dogs are injured or killed every year from jumping from the bed of a moving pickup, or from being thrown from the truck at a sudden stop or in an accident.

Eliminating Nervousness and Car Sickness

Car sickness and fearful behavior in the car represent cycles of behavior. Your dog anticipates that the car will take him somewhere frightening, so he's terrified to get in the car. If he has been ill in the car in the past, he may feel ill as soon as he gets into the vehicle. It's your job to help your dog disassociate riding in the car from these triggers for his fear and sickness.

How to Help Your Dog Enjoy Going for a Ride

1. Just hang out. Familiarize your dog with the car without taking him on trips. When you're getting groceries out of the trunk, have him tag along. Let him "help" you wash the car in the driveway. He'll learn that going near the car isn't dangerous. Periodically put him in his crate in the car, and then take him out right away. Give him a treat and tell him he's terrific. Eventually, he'll learn that the crate in the car isn't going to make him sick. Once he's going into his crate without fear, put him in the crate and turn on the engine, letting the car run a couple of minutes. Let him out of the crate, and give him a treat and play with him. Repeat this until he's calm when the car starts up.

2. Drive around the block. Take your dog on short trips just around the block. When you're done with the trip, again praise and play with your dog. It shouldn't take long for him to be calm in this situation.

3. Take short trips. Once the dog isn't afraid of going around the block, start going on short trips to pleasant places. One reason many dogs fear going in the car is that every trip in their experience has been traumatic. Do most of your dog's car trips end up at the veterinarian's office? If every trip you ever took in a car was to a place where a stranger gave you shots or practiced surgery on you, you wouldn't like travel too well, either. Puppies who have traveled by car or plane long distances to their new homes often have special troubles with car sickness as well and might display symptoms of anxiety until they become accustomed to the car.

Take your dog on short car trips to local parks and other places he enjoys. Get out and play with him once you arrive at the park. It won't take long for your dog to realize that most destinations in the car are to fabulous places, and he'll start to relax. His nervousness, including car sickness, will almost always end.

4. Give your dog a view. Some dogs are less likely to be nauseous if they can see out the windows. If nausea is an ongoing problem, try using a wire crate or a doggie seatbelt. Also try putting the dog in the front seat of the car, where there is less motion.

5. Minimize the problem. Until your dog has overcome his car sickness, help minimize the problem. Don't feed him the day he's going on a trip (but do be sure he has plenty of water). He'll be less likely to throw up if he hasn't eaten anything. If he frequently defecates in the car, give him a baby glycerin suppository before the trip. (The specifics of dealing with nervous defecation are covered in chapter eight.)

Using the techniques of gradually acclimating your dog to car trips will almost always eliminate the problem of car sickness. It's worth it to take the time to teach your dog to enjoy his rides in the car—it's part of the process of turning him into a great friend and traveling buddy.

REAPING THE REWARDS

You've now exposed your dog to a variety of environments. He still may not be too thrilled with the idea of leaving the house, but at least he has found that every trip outside the front door doesn't always end up at the veterinarian's office or the animal shelter. He'll learn to look forward to your walks, and he'll soon jump happily into the car to go for a ride. When you arrive at a new place to explore, he'll be eager to get out and smell the smells and see the sights. With a little more time and practice, you'll give him the gift that every dog deserves: the opportunity to enjoy the world around him.

Weazie: Sweet Victories

Weazie is a brave little buckaroo.

Shannon Chenault remembers the first day she saw Weazie. Shannon was making a sales call at a customer's home, where a little black mixed-breed dog was cowering under a table, trying to avoid the family's three rowdy boys.

Weazie's name was originally Weasel. The 4-year-old dog had a nasty case of fleas and was allergic to the pests; she was constantly biting and chewing at herself, and she had patches of missing hair. When people reached to pet Weazie, she responded with submissive urination. "I just told myself over and over, 'I can't save them all,'" Shannon remembers.

Nearly every time Shannon made a sales call at that house, she would find Weazie hiding under a piece of furniture, especially if the boys were around. "Weazie would wait for an opportune time, run across the room, leap into my lap, and look at me as if to plead, 'Please take me home,'" Shannon says. "I reminded myself again that I couldn't save every dog on the planet. Then the owners told me they were going to get rid of Weazie or have her put to sleep because she'd bitten the boys.

I could tell that deep down she was a really nice little dog, so I said I would help them find a home for Weazie."

Life with Weazie

Shannon succeeded in finding a new home for the dog. "I told the adoptive home that Weazie was going to need a lot of rehab," she says. "I thought they knew what they were getting into. Apparently they didn't, because they gave me back the dog a few days later."

Rather than returning Weazie to her original home, Shannon decided to keep the dog long enough to provide sufficient rehab to make her adoptable. Shannon says with a laugh, "During this time we bought her a collar, and then a leash, and then we got her a rabies shot. After three months I turned to my husband and asked, 'Are we keeping her? If so, we really ought to get her licensed.' And so Weazie became our dog."

Life with Weazie wasn't easy. Her submissive urination continued for some time. If Shannon raised her voice, even to another dog, Weazie would run out of the room, afraid.

Shannon began to work slowly with Weazie. "The first thing I taught her was to sit and stay," recalls Shannon. "We worked in the house—she would have been too nervous in the yard. I could get her to sit, but she'd move if I took my hands off her. After practicing regularly for three weeks, I was able to take my hand 2 inches away from her body."

Practice and Persistence Pay

Shannon continued to train Weazie, first in the house, then in the yard and finally in a park. It took six months of daily practice before Shannon could stand 6 feet away from Weazie for a sit-stay. Finally, after half a year of work, Weazie had enough confidence to enter training class. Throughout Weazie's training, Shannon focused on positive methods. She relied heavily on praise and reward, and the dog learned to enjoy the work.

Shannon pursued formal training with Weazie to help the little dog gain confidence. "I never thought too much about how much progress we were making," admits Shannon. "There were so many little accomplishments along the way. Those were enough for me. I never thought about competing or obedience titles. Suddenly, I found myself in the obedience ring with this dog, and Weazie earned a U-C.D. (United Kennel Club Companion Dog title)."

To earn a U-C.D. title, Weazie had to heel on and off the leash, jump over a hurdle and come to Shannon, stand for examination while a judge touched her, do a long down-stay while another dog worked in the ring and do a long sit-stay in a line of other dogs. Weazie had to pass the test on three different occasions at dog shows, where she was surrounded by other dogs.

Shannon explains, "It was a long road for Weazie, so her victory was super-sweet. She was so proud of herself—she was sure she'd won the Nobel Prize!"

Shannon also began training Weazie in agility, basically an obstacle course in which the dogs jump over hurdles, run through above-ground tunnels and climb over objects. Shannon never expected Weazie to enter an agility competition, but today, Weazie has an Elite Jumpers title and a Novice Gamblers title from the North American Dog Agility Council. "She loves to jump!" says Shannon. "When I'm ready to practice her agility, I say to Weazie, 'Want to work?' and she runs out to our agility practice area."

Weazie has also passed the AKC Canine Good Citizen test and is a certified therapy dog.

"I look at where Weazie started and look at where she is now," says Shannon, with tears in her eyes. "She's overcome so many things. I was even proud of her the day she could manage to do a sit-stay and let me take two steps back. Weazie will try to do anything I ask of her. She may not be able to accomplish it, but she will always try. There isn't a sweeter dog on the whole planet. She has overcome one obstacle after another—Weazie is a brave little buckaroo."

Little Victories

Despite her success, Shannon is quick to point out that some behaviors still linger even after four years. For instance, Weazie still doesn't like loud noises. Whenever Shannon knows there's going to be a loud sound, she tells Weazie "big noise" so the dog can prepare herself. Other situations are still too intimidating for Weazie to undertake. For example, the noise and movement of running over a teeter-totter in agility competition is too much for Weazie. "She'll stand there and wag her tail, as if to say 'I want to.' But sometimes she just can't," Shannon says. "I let her know that I'm pleased with her for just trying."

Shannon also has plenty of advice for people considering adopting a fearful dog. "Have reasonable expectations," she says. "An abused dog with hang-ups isn't going to learn at the same rate that a confident puppy will. If you think the dog will, you're going to face disappointment. Be ready to put a lot of time and patience into the dog, and to take one day at a time. Also be ready for a ton of joy. If you go in with a positive attitude and take one step at a time, it will be worth every minute you spend with the dog."

Of course, patience also comes in handy when starting out on the long road to improvement. "People often say to me that I have a lot of patience with Weazie, but I don't think of it that way," says Shannon. "I have lower standards for Weazie than I do for some of my other dogs because she's had so much to overcome. I celebrate our small victories, not overlook them. I just appreciate what Weazie gives to me. Her little victories are like little gifts from God."

After my interview with Shannon at an agility competition at which Weazie is entered, I watch as the small dog tears through the course, leaping over hurdles and speeding through tunnels. The crowd loves her performance and cheers the little dog on. At the end of her run, Weazie looks over at the crowd and leaps over an extra two hurdles, her tail wagging with exhilaration. When Shannon and Weazie exit from the ring, Weazie goes up to several of Shannon's friends, expecting the congratulatory pats that are forthcoming. Like all of Weazie's victories, this one is sweet.

Chapter Three

Little Things Mean a Lot

Wow, we love flags!

You interact with your dog in thousands of little ways every day. Those little interactions, and the underlying messages they give to your dog, have enormous power to heal or to harm your timid friend.

Whether you've just brought home your fearful dog or you've had her for years, today is the day to start the transition that will change your dog's life. It doesn't matter whether your dog is a shy six-month-old puppy who has been loved and well cared for since the day she was born, or whether she is an abused, older dog you rescued. Your dog can't get better until you set the tone and make change happen. Communicating confidence to your dog doesn't take a second of extra time. The use of your voice, body posture and general tone you set with your dog have enormous power to heal.

Try these little steps that can bring about big changes in your shy dog.

DON'T REWARD SHY BEHAVIOR

Never pet your dog when she's acting shy and fearful. If you do, you're reinforcing the fearful behavior. Instead, ignore it. Pretend the dog isn't shivering. Disregard the puddle of submissive urination. These are uncontrollable acts at this time from your dog. Over time, these behaviors will disappear.

Reward the behavior you want. Pet your dog when she's acting in a more outgoing, bold manner. Give her a treat when she's being calm in a new situation. Ignoring shy behavior and rewarding bold behavior will help the dog learn to act more confident.

Of course, this is easier to say than to do. When a loud noise startles your dog, the most natural thing in the world is to hold her in your arms and reassure her that she'll be all right. You have to break the habit of your own behavior before your dog can learn to break the habit of hers.

The next time you hear that loud noise and your dog jumps, smile at her and look relaxed. In a happy, confident voice say, "Don't worry, Princess, it's just noise." When you give the dog no cue that she should be afraid, it will greatly diminish her fear reaction.

Examine your body language, how you hold your leash and how you interact with your dog. For her to believe that she has nothing to fear, you must demonstrate daily through your body language that she isn't a victim. This will be difficult at first, because you know how hard life is for her. But her life will remain hard for her to bear until she begins to view herself as a confident dog—she can do that only if she sees confidence reflected in your eyes.

Give Non-threatening Greetings

Never approach your dog with your hand stretched out above her head. Placing your arm above a dog's head is the most threatening possible approach you can give a fearful dog. Instead of reaching out to pet the top of her head, reach down and scratch her chin or chest. This will make a big difference in your dog's ability to relax with you. Make sure other people who pet your dog do the same.

How much difference can this little thing make? One person told me about a dog who submissively urinated every time someone petted her. Upon a friend's suggestion, the owner stopped reaching over the dog's head. That minor adjustment completely solved the dog's submissive urination problem! Whether your dog shows her anxiety through urination, cringing or just a disinterest in being petted, a non-threatening chin or chest scratch can increase your dog's quality of life.

Don't Necessarily Squat

Countless dog books will tell you to squat down to the dog's level when greeting a shy dog. Those countless books aren't necessarily right, though. For many shy dogs, a squatting human is very intimidating.

As one experienced dog trainer explained it, a Great Dane would probably see a squatting person as very non-threatening, since by squatting the person becomes smaller than the dog and makes the dog feel dominant. A mid-sized dog, such as a Golden Retriever, might see a squatting person as an equal. To a small dog, however, the change in shape can be terrifying. In addition, some dogs don't like the thought of a human transforming into some strange, new shape. For this dog, the human isn't behaving in normal human ways, and that makes her more nervous. Instead of wanting to get closer to that person, the fearful dog is even more motivated to pull away. If the dog is a fear-biter, the person squatting on the ground is in considerable danger of a receiving a nasty bite.

Twice I have seen otherwise sane and knowledgeable dog lovers lie down on the ground to reassure a small, fearful dog. In both cases, the dogs were clearly disturbed by this odd human behavior.

Watch your dog to see what postures make her feel most comfortable. If a squatting person makes her feel confident, then squat. If an upright posture seems more to her liking, stay on your own two feet.

As your dog becomes confident and you begin desensitizing her to things that make her nervous, expose her to people who are squatting and rolling around on the ground. Your dog will probably never be impressed by these human antics, but she can become used to them over time.

Don't Stare

Direct, strong eye contact is a dominant behavior in dogs. Avoid staring at your dog, and never force her to look into your eyes. When looking at your dog, use a soft expression, not a penetrating stare. With your soft, gentle looks of love, your shy dog will find you much more approachable.

Keep the Paws on the Ground

Look at your dog's feet. If she's a small dog, are her paws on the ground when you go for your walk? Are you carrying her instead of letting the poor dog walk? Put the dog on the ground! Not only does this get your dog the exercise she needs, but your signal to her when you carry her is that she's in danger. It's scary to put your little dog on the ground of this big world, but remember that you're adding to the fearful quality of her life when you hold her. Soon you'll notice that she acts more confident when she's walking than when she's being carried. She'll learn she's a real dog and can have a real life.

Of course, use good sense with a small dog. Little dogs are in real danger from attacks and even overly enthusiastic play from a large dog. If a situation puts your dog in danger, of course you should carry her. One owner of a small dog said, "My dog must always know that I would never put her in a situation in which another dog will harm her. One breach of trust, and we'd have to start all over." It's your job as your dog's protector to decide if the situation puts your dog in real danger. If the situation is safe but the dog is nervous, let her learn to walk on her own four feet.

Get There Early

Nervous dogs take longer than more confident dogs to relax in a new situation. Go to new places before everyone else shows up so that your dog will have time to get used to the environment before she has to get used to all the people. Arrive at training class 15 minutes before everyone else, or be the first one to show up at the family picnic. Not only does this give your dog time to get acclimated to a new place, but in dog terms, the first dog on the scene has "dibs" on the territory. From this standpoint, arriving early gives your dog a better sense of confidence to be on "her" turf. Allowing your dog a bit of extra time to get her bearings may take a few minutes from your day, but it will make any stressful experience for your dog a lot easier for you both to bear.

Keep a Regular Routine

All dogs like routine and structure, but nervous dogs in particular are reassured by a regular routine. Plan walks, mealtimes, grooming and other daily activities at about the same time each day. These occurrences will be less nerve-wracking to your dog if she knows when to expect them.

Be Consistent

Consistency is the key in training any dog. "Heel" should always mean the exact same position. "Stay" should always mean that the dog mustn't move from the exact spot where she was left. It's hard enough for a dog to have to figure out the words another species is saying to her, but it's totally unfair if the meanings of the words change constantly. Imagine taking a foreign language course and having an instructor invent different meanings each time you practiced a word!

Although consistency is important for all dogs, it's especially important for fearful dogs. These are dogs who want to follow, not lead. They don't like risk, and they try hard to do the right thing. When you are inconsistent, you undermine your dog's faith in you. The rules in your home should be very clear—and should be gently, lovingly and consistently enforced.

Over time, your dog's reliance on your consistent structure will translate into trust in you. Such trust doesn't come automatically in a nervous dog, though. Your dog needs the certainty of consistent structure and routine to bridge her fear.

TAKE THE LEAD (NO PUN INTENDED)

Establish yourself as your dog's pack leader. She's less likely to be fearful if she knows she has a strong leader.

Dogs aren't just people in fur coats. As a human, your levels of fear and anxiety would probably increase if someone walked in and took control of your life. For a dog, however, this reduces her fears. Dogs look to their pack leaders for security, food and warmth. They want their leaders to make the decisions for the pack.

When I first got my fearful dog, Goldie, I behaved in just the opposite manner of what she needed in a pack leader. During my years of providing housing and social services to people, I was very careful to provide people with choices. When I was working with a person who was very insecure, I'd give that person a sense of control of the situation. I'd make it clear that he or she had several options and could choose among those options. I'd back off and let the person make his or her own decisions.

When I tried to use the same technique with Goldie, it was a disaster. I basically treated Goldie as I would a fearful human: I let her make decisions. When we'd go for a walk, I let her decide which direction to go. I'd let her make up her own mind about how close to go to people or to other dogs. She grew increasingly overwhelmed and fearful.

Fearful dogs are not reassured by making choices—instead, this adds to their terror. If you provide leadership, however, your dog will calm down enormously. When you give your dog too many choices, the dog perceives you as a weak pack leader. An aggressive dog would try to take over at this point, but a timid dog will become more shy because she doesn't have the security of a strong leader to protect her.

Goldie's view of our walks differed from mine. In her world, her pack leader (me) was indecisive and ineffective. I was forcing the 6-pound dog to take on the pack leadership role. Yet Goldie never wanted to be the pack leader. She wanted to be a follower. The leadership role overwhelmed her and reduced her trust in me.

I learned that I had to set the direction for Goldie. Now I tell her "this way," and she can follow. I watch for signs of things that interest her. If she wants to stop and sniff at a tree, she'll let me know. If I see that she's looking curiously at a bird, I'll walk in that direction. I make sure that she gets her needs met—but her needs are met as a follower, not as a pack leader. Her relief when I became a proper leader was enormous: She wanted the grown-up human rather than the 6-pound dog to take charge!

Strong leadership doesn't mean abusive or rough behavior, though. The dog is looking for a confident and reassuring boss; she doesn't need a human in her life who will give her more reason to fear.

MAKE THE DOG PART OF THE HOUSEHOLD

Fearful dogs often want to hide away from everyone else. Although your dog (like every other dog) needs a safe bed or crate where she can go when she wants to sleep or relax, she also needs to be kept in an active part of the household. Put her bed in a room where the action is. If everyone in the family (whether your family is just you or includes a dozen people) is in the living room, make sure the dog is in the living room with you. Don't let her live a shadowy existence, hiding at the far corners of the house away from all of you.

One person who was interviewed for this book reported, "When I first got my dog, I set up her bed in the far corner of the house to give her privacy. Then I realized I never saw her. I moved her bed to the middle of the action. Now she participates in the household with me. It has made a difference in her behavior." Communicate to the dog that she belongs in the family by physically placing here there.

Give Your Dog an Honored Place

Fearful dogs know their place in the hierarchy: the bottom. Every encounter is frightening and requires active submission.

Communicate to your dog that she's an important part of the pack. Praise her, talk to her, admire her, groom her, make a fuss over her. These daily reminders of her importance will go a long way in her rehabilitation into a confident, happy dog.

DON'T "ENABLE"

Those of us who have worked in the social services have learned that we don't help our clients by giving them excuses that allow them to behave in their old, dysfunctional ways. Treating clients as victims and doing things for them that they are perfectly capable of doing for themselves, perpetuates the cycle of failure in their lives. This practice of setting up people for failure by assuming that they will never be able to fend for themselves is called *enabling*. We help people most when we let them stand on their own two feet: In this case, you need to let your dog stand on her own four paws.

Starting today, don't enable your dog's fearful behaviors. Envision the cheerful, curious, confident dog you want your dog to be. Then treat her as if she were that animal. After all, the manner in which you treat your dog will determine how your dog views her role in the world.

This means talking to your dog in a happy, calm tone of voice. To a dog, your baby talk and cooing sound like a whine. No more whining! Your cooing voice signals to the dog that she has something to fear. When you see a flag snapping in the wind, don't coo, "Poor Princess, that nasty old flag up there won't hurt my baby." Instead, in a happy, confident voice say, "Look at that, Princess. It's a flag. Wow, we love flags!" Princess may not be convinced the first time, but the next time she sees a flag snapping in the wind, she'll have a bit less fear.

Ask your family members and friends to listen to you when you talk to your dog. Of course you should sound affectionate. But are you speaking with the same enthusiastic tone you'd give to a bold, strong dog? Or are you reserving a special little voice for your dog who's a victim? Remember, you're doing your dog no favors by allowing her to remain a victim. Speak to her as if she were the well-adjusted, confident dog you want her to be.

DON'T BARK

Some people—particularly some men—have the opposite problem. They don't whine at their dogs; they bark orders at them. A brusque, loud voice sounds like a challenge to a shy dog—and the last thing a shy dog wants is a challenge because she'll do anything to appease you. In fact, a common response to a brusque voice is submissive urination. Listen again to how you sound, and ask other people to listen to you. Your voice should be confident—but also happy and friendly. Soft, sure tones are what you're striving for.

MAKE SURE YOUR DOG IS SAFE IN HER HOME

Your dog can't get better if she isn't safe in her own home. Is every member of the family kind to the dog? If you have a spouse or a live-in partner who hurts or yells at the dog or at people whom the dog loves, you have to part with either the relationship or the dog. (I'd suggest keeping the dog!)

Are your children kind to the dog, even when you aren't at home? Kids can be a great part of a dog's healing, as long as they are gentle and play with the dog appropriately. In fact, a key component to many dogs' recoveries has been the loving, joyful play of children. However, some dogs aren't able to adjust to a noisy, busy household full of children. Small, fearful dogs can be an especially bad combination with children under the age of 6. Honestly examine your home. Are the adults and children gentle and understanding enough to help your nervous dog? If not, you may not have the best household for the dog.

It's not enabling to make sure that your timid dog isn't being abused, harassed or pushed to the point of exhaustion; it's simply responsible dog ownership that communicates to the dog that you are her protector and that she can relax.

DON'T LOSE YOUR TEMPER

Your shy dog can make you feel very frustrated. One day she'll be happy and confident; the next day she'll be shaking and afraid. Sometimes you'll believe she's never going to get better, and you'll want to scream. Instead, bite your lip, count to 10 and stay calm. Your dog isn't acting shy to spite you; it's her nature to be shy. Losing your temper with your dog never helps; it always makes the problem worse.

TALK TO YOUR DOG

Your dog will pick up the meaning of many words if you talk to her, and your dog will be a smarter, better pet as a result. Especially after you have trained your dog, she'll learn to pick up words quickly. It's amazing how many words a dog learns just by associating what you say with what she observes. Can it be useful? Sure. In such cases, you're training your dog with absolutely no effort.

Here are just a few of the words my dogs learned from listening to me while I talked to them around the house and on our walks:

- **"Say hi."** We'd go on walks and I'd see someone I knew, so I'd say to the dogs, "Let's go say hi." It took very little time for them to learn that "say hi" means they get to go greet someone. My shy dog has learned that she doesn't have to fear anyone who rates a "say hi" from me.

- **"Look."** I didn't even realize that I'd say "look" when I saw something interesting. Now when I tell my dogs "look" and point to an object, they'll run up to that object. One of the most difficult commands in dog training is to teach a dog to go out away from you to find things, and my dogs taught themselves the command from my casual conversations.

- **Object names.** My dogs recognize the names of many things, such as "bird" (which they want to hunt) or the names of their toys.

- **"Time for bed."** When I tell the dogs it's time for bed, they trot into the bedroom. (Of course, they've also trained me. If I'm up too late writing or reading, they come nudge me and tell me it's past my bedtime. This training thing is a two-way street!)

If you talk to your dog around the house and out on your walks, you'll find that your dog has learned more than you would have thought possible. This kind of ongoing communication also strengthens your bond and helps your dog in more formal training.

TEACH "CHECK IT OUT"

"Check it out" is a cue you can give your dog to let her know an object is safe. Teach this by putting a little treat on the floor and saying, "Check it out." The dog will soon learn to associate the phrase "check it out" with the pleasant experience of finding this little tidbit. Then begin to hide the tidbit under a bit of cloth or under a paper cup. When the dog checks out the cloth or cup, she'll find the hidden treat. "Check it out" will soon become her favorite phrase!

Once she understands the phrase, use it to introduce your shy dog to items that make her a little nervous. If she begins to shy away from an object, say "check it out" and put your hand on the object. She'll sniff the object to see if something delicious is lurking beneath its surface. Praise the dog for her boldness and give her a treat if you've got one. Be sure to tell your dog to "check it out" only if you know the object is absolutely safe. If you tell your dog to check out an object that falls apart and frightens her, you've broken your bond of trust.

Use "Check it out" to introduce your shy dog to items
that make her a little nervous.

TOUCH YOUR DOG

Many shy dogs don't like petting. Dogs who have been abused have an understandable fear of human contact. Many dogs who are averse to petting, however, have never been hurt by a human hand. Touch violates their sense of personal safety and triggers a "flight or fight" response. The solution is to desensitize your dog by gently and consistently touching her. Scratch her on the chest. Gently tug on her ears, starting at the base and working out toward the tips. Rub her tummy.

One particularly effective technique is Tellington Touch (also called TTouch). This technique consists primarily of gently moving your fingers in small clockwise circles over your dog's skin. TTouch practitioners believe the technique helps to re-educate an animals' cellular memory, erasing memories of fear and pain.

My dog, Goldie, who has never really liked petting, loves TTouch. Every night when I settle down to give her TTouch, she wags her tail and jumps on my lap, eager for the treatment.

In addition to TTouch, dog massage books are available, or people who are trained in human massage can give you tips for massaging your nervous dog. The results can be very rewarding for your dog and will add to your bond of communication with your pet.

EXERCISE YOUR DOG

Make sure your dog gets plenty of exercise. Teach her to play fetch. Go jogging together. Take long walks in your favorite park. Join a dog play group. Everyone feels less anxiety after they've had a good workout — your dog included.

TRY RESCUE REMEDY

Bach™ Flower Essences are homeopathic remedies available at many health food stores. Many owners of shy dogs report that Rescue Remedy, one of Bach's products, helps calm a worried dog. Just put a couple of drops of Rescue Remedy in your dog's water every day. In tiny doses, the remedy won't hurt your dog—it just might help.

BE PATIENT

Recovery doesn't happen overnight. Major change requires a commitment over time. Behavior changes are much like the incoming tide; the good days gradually get better, and the bad days gradually get less problematic. None of us gets better while a stopwatch ticks in our ear, proclaiming a deadline on our recovery. Your dog isn't going to wake up one morning and suddenly be cured. She needs the freedom to work through her fearfulness at her own pace.

Your dog's recovery may be so gradual that you won't notice the profound changes taking place in her behavior. Every once in a while, remind yourself of how she reacted to a situation six months ago, and compare it to how she reacts to the same situation today. You'll realize just how much your patient work has paid off. If you have a video camera, look at videos from just a few months ago. You'll be stunned by the change.

Accept the fact that your fearful dog will perform tasks in public more slowly than her more outgoing counterparts. This doesn't mean that your dog is less intelligent than the other dogs in your neighborhood, though. As one person describes his risk-averse dog, "He doesn't want to make a mistake or put himself in a position that seems dangerous to him. He learns a training exercise faster than most of the other dogs in his class. He just takes a while before he can make himself perform the task in class or other high-stress places."

Every person who was interviewed for this book stressed that it takes longer to convince a fearful dog to perform a task in public than it does to get a bold dog to perform the same task in public. Some shy dogs learn very quickly; they're just nervous in front of an audience. They're like the shy child who knows a poem backward and forward—and then freezes when required to recite the poem in class. It's frustrating to know that your dog understands how to do a task but that she's just too insecure to actually perform.

Dogs who have been neglected or abused may learn noticeably slower than other dogs. In their pasts, human actions have been inconsistent or even dangerous. It takes longer for these dogs to understand that your words and actions aren't random; they're cues for the dog to behave in a certain way. Whether your dog learns a little more slowly than other dogs or just has stage fright, training is a slower process than it is for bold, outgoing dogs. Some days you will need infinite patience.

Starting today, resolve to have the patience that it takes to bring your dog out of her shell. Accept the fact that your dog will learn to change slowly. Viewed one way, training a fearful dog is a lot of work: It takes two or three times as long to teach a fearful dog to execute a basic exercise in public as it does to teach the same exercise to a confident dog. Viewed another way, however, working with a fearful dog is no more time-consuming than working with any other dog. I work with my shy dog the same amount of time each day that I work with my bold, outgoing dog. My bold dog learns more exercises in the same amount of time, but I don't put in a different amount of time per day. Each dog learns at her own pace.

Love your dog enough to give her the freedom to learn at her own pace. Love her enough not to compare her with other dogs. The trust and love you receive in return will more than make up for the effort you've spent.

Nellie:
A Case of Notorious Neglect

ℛ

Nellie (right) loves to play with her friend Norman, the Beagle.

In rural Clatsop County, Oregon, Vikki Kittles lived in a school bus with 117 dogs, 4 cats and 2 chickens. On April 15, 1993, Clatsop County Animal Control Services seized the animals. They were in terrible condition: The dogs were coated with urine and feces, and they had developed sores from lying in their own filth. Most of the dogs were malnourished; some were near starvation. Many suffered from a variety of parasites, including ringworm, heartworm and giardia.

Nellie was one of the dogs rescued that day.

"I couldn't let that woman keep those animals in that school bus under those dreadful conditions," says Tommie Brunick, the Clatsop County Animal Control Services Division supervisor. "I knew we had to try to save them."

Tommie remembers that many people advised her to euthanize all the dogs. A lot of so-called "experts" said the animals would never be adoptable. But Tommie was determined to save as many animals as she could.

Vikki Kittles maneuvered through the legal system for 22 months after the dogs were seized before she was finally found guilty of animal neglect and sentenced to jail time. During much of that time, the dogs were denied medical care because Kittles didn't believe in veterinary treatment. She wouldn't allow the dogs to be adopted out to new homes, and the animal shelter had no legal recourse but to hold them in kennels and eventually foster care until Kittles was found guilty.

"We really worked with the dogs during those 22 months," says Tommie. "We had a full-time person whose job was just to help them learn to respond to human touch and teach them how to relate to people. We also had so many wonderful people from our community helping out. It really showed me how much a small community can accomplish for animals once people understand what's at stake."

One Lucky Dog

When the court declared that Vikki Kittles had no custody rights to the dogs, the animals were ready to be adopted. Because there were too many dogs for the small communities in Clatsop County to absorb, the dogs were placed with shelters throughout the state of Oregon. Officials prepared personality profiles of each of the dogs so that the shelter staff could let prospective owners know what they were getting into.

Almost two years to the day after the raid on the bus, Jean Kunkle adopted Nellie from a humane society in the Willamette Valley.

Now a year and a half after the adoption, I meet Jean and Nellie on a warm summer day in a grassy park. Devotion to Jean sparkles in Nellie's soft brown eyes as the pretty mixed-breed dog looks up every few moments just to be sure Jean isn't going anywhere. Nellie's sleek brown and white coat is glossy; her lithe body and well-defined muscles demonstrate that she receives plenty of healthy exercise.

Jean recalls the first days of owning Nellie. "I called her Nellie because she was such a nervous Nellie—I guess I could have called her shrinking Violet."

Although Jean can laugh now, she feared she would have to return Nellie to the humane society during the first few weeks. "Nellie was too afraid to go out in my backyard by herself. I had to take her out on walks because she was too nervous to go to the bathroom in the yard. She wouldn't eat or drink water when I was in the room. She shook in fear."

Jean looks over at Nellie as the dog contentedly chews a bone. "I was petrified it wasn't going to work out. A lot of people told me I should just take her back, that it wasn't worth it. Now it's hard to believe I could ever have thought of giving her up. I'm so glad I have her. I didn't know that a dog could be such good company."

A Social Butterfly

Jean began taking Nellie on walks, both in her neighborhood and in the local parks. At first, Nellie was frightened on the walks and would shake or try to pull back and run away. But Jean persevered. Now Nellie enjoys going hiking and exploring new places. Jean also found a group of dog owners with well-behaved dogs who play together. At first, Nellie wouldn't go near the other dogs. Now she enjoys playing with the less imposing dogs, especially the puppies. Recently, she has been socializing with the bold, adult dogs, as well.

Nellie has also begun to do well in training class. As we chat, Jean demonstrates some of Nellie's abilities. Nellie comes, sits and lies downs with precision and quickness, all while looking at Jean with adoring eyes.

"Nellie's proud of her work," explains Jean. "When I call her in practice, she'll race to me like the dog in the Mighty Dog® commercials. Recently, all the dogs in our training class were required to do a long down in a big huddle with each other, and I had to stand several feet away. Nellie was apprehensive, but she did great. Now she's learning to jump hurdles in class and she's really enjoying it. I feel like we've accomplished a lot, especially since the people at the humane society told me that she'd probably never be able to learn obedience very well."

A Work in Progress

Jean also has her share of advice for people considering adopting their own nervous Nellies: "Don't give up. Give it at least a month to work out, and believe that your dog won't act like that forever. It's frustrating sometimes, but over time your dog will change."

Jean also encourages owners of fearful dogs to seek out advice and help from experts on dog behavior. Jean herself went to the humane society at least once a week to ask questions.

She also got some help simply by asking questions of others. For example, Nellie developed a terrible fear of leashes. She'd see her leash lying on the ground and would run away in terror. When Jean told her veterinarian about the problem, the doctor suggested leaving a treat next to the leash and making Nellie come to the leash to get the treat. When Jean went to work, she left the leash on the floor with a treat right next to it. When she returned home, the treat was gone. Now Jean ties the treat up inside the leash. When she gets home, Nellie has unsnarled the leash to get the treat. Through this routine, Nellie has begun to see the leash as a source of treats rather than as a scary object. She's still working through her fear of leashes when she's wearing one, but she's definitely making progress.

Indeed, Nellie is a work in progress. Her confidence continues to improve, and Jean and Nellie's efforts are beginning to translate into concrete changes in Nellie's behavior and quality of life. "At times I don't see the progress," says Jean, "and then one of my friends or neighbors will say, 'I can't believe the difference in that dog.' The improvement is so gradual, I don't always see it."

Nellie's improvements have often been in decreasing fearful habits rather than totally eliminating the habits. "She used to shake like an earthquake," says Jean. "Now the same situation may just cause her front leg to quiver."

Nellie's Happy Ending

For a long time, Nellie's life was defined by neglect, and nothing can take away the time she spent in a filthy, excrement-filled bus full of sick dogs. But because a small animal shelter was willing to put its resources on the line for a busload of dogs, Nellie got a chance. And because of Jean, Nellie leads a happy, interesting life.

As I watch Nellie playing in the grass at Jean's feet, the bond between the two of them is obvious. The dog watches Jean's every move and responds joyfully to Jean's verbal cues—in essence, Nellie's life is being redefined.

Today, Nellie's world is one of security, learned trust and returned love. A year and a half after Nellie's adoption, the faith of an animal shelter and all of Jean's hard work are just beginning to pay off. Nellie's confidence and zest for life are increasing on a daily basis. Most importantly, she isn't a victim anymore.

Chapter Four

Training: The Best Gift You Can Give Your Dog

Your dog can succeed beyond your wildest dreams.

Love your dog, play with your dog, believe in your dog—but most importantly, train your dog. It's almost impossible for a dog to overcome fearful and shy behavior without training.

Dog training has made great leaps forward in the last 20 years. Throughout the country, professional dog trainers and behaviorists use positive, cruelty-free techniques that are a joy for both dog and owner.

Positive training is the ultimate in developing a profound, loving relationship with your dog. It's two-way communication between dog and owner that people who've never owned a trained dog can't really imagine.

Once you learn to communicate with your dog through training, it really is like living with Lassie. You and your dog will have a bond that's different than any other relationship you can have. I promise you that, after living with a well-trained dog, you will never be willing to live with an untrained dog again.

POSITIVE TRAINING WILL CHANGE YOUR DOG'S LIFE

The role training can play in transforming your timid dog was best explained by Barbara Griffin, the owner of Challenge, a Golden Retriever: "You can't just tell your dog to stop being fearful—it doesn't work. But you can teach him to do exercises that will overcome his basic instinct to act afraid. When you have an overly friendly dog, you don't say, 'Don't be friendly!' You teach him to sit and stay when people come over. His learned behavior overcomes his desire to jump on people. It's the same with a fearful dog. When he learns to sit and stay, or to heel, he learns to perform the task instead of act afraid."

WHY TRAINING IS ESPECIALLY IMPORTANT FOR FEARFUL DOGS

- **Builds confidence.** Training will build your dog's confidence. The early stages of dog training are small bits of accomplishment. When your dog learns to sit, he has accomplished something. When he learns to come on command, he has accomplished something. It feels good for both dogs and humans to make tangible progress.

Within the first few weeks of training, you'll notice an improvement in your dog's temperament. The achievable tasks in training will help your dog develop a focus that will spill over into how he reacts to the rest of his environment.

It's ironic that many people believe training will break a dog's spirit. Especially with the new, positive training methods available today, just the opposite is true. Training will make your fearful dog more playful, bold and assertive.

- **Teaches communication.** Positive training teaches your dog the concept of communication. Your dog will learn your words have meaning, and he'll discover your actions aren't just random.

This is particularly important for a dog who has been abused or neglected. These types of dogs have led lives in which human action was incomprehensible. For an abused dog, human behavior was unpredictable and dangerous. Sometimes the dog's behavior may have been ignored or even encouraged; the next time that same behavior may have resulted in a beating. Neglected dogs have often shut down communication with people altogether. After all, when the dog communicated that he needed to exercise or he needed attention, the human in his life didn't respond at all. Why should he believe that there is any purpose to a human's words or actions?

Training can change all that. Once the dog sees consistency and reward for communicating in his training routines, he'll begin to apply that lesson to other aspects of his relationship with you.

- **Modifies flight or fight.** Training changes your dog's reaction to the flight or fight response. When something creates fear in your dog, that stimulus triggers your dog's most basic instinct. The dog will either have an overwhelming desire to run away from the object of his fear, or, if he feels cornered, to fight.

Through training, your dog learns to focus on the task at hand. When he's doing a sit-stay and there's a loud noise near him, his first reaction may be to run. However, if he's trained, the flight or fight response will be overridden by the need to stay focused on the task he's performing. As the dog gains confidence through training, he'll learn to ignore noises and other distractions that at one time would have created terror. He'll gain a sense of control over his own world that may someday save his life.

● **Increases intelligence.** Training will increase your dog's intelligence. Many studies have shown that animals kept in environments that lack stimulation have physically less brain capacity than animals that live in environments rich in activity. Additional studies have demonstrated that adding activity to an animal's environment actually increases the physical capacity of the animal's brain. This increase in brain power can happen anytime during the animal's lifetime.

Training will not just teach your dog specific exercises. The use of his brain through training will increase his ability to learn other things. This is particularly important for dogs who have been neglected and haven't had their fair share of mental and physical stimulation. Training is their chance to mentally catch up with other dogs.

FINDING THE RIGHT TRAINING CLASS

Now that you believe that training is essential for your dog, it's time to find a good class.

Why a class? Can't you just get one of the countless dog-training books or videos and train from that? For a problem dog, the insights and information you will get from an experienced, capable trainer can never be replicated by reading a book. An experienced trainer will know when it's time to encourage your dog to try something new, and when it's time to hold back. He or she can point out when you're enabling your dog, and when you're expecting too much of him. On the days you're feeling frustrated, your trainer will point out the progress you've made. When one technique doesn't work, an experienced trainer will have half a dozen other techniques to try.

Many owners of fearful dogs don't like the idea of taking their dogs to a class full of nasty, large, untrained dogs. Isn't it better to take private lessons from a trainer? Sometimes. If a class is too overwhelming at first, it might be a good idea to take some private lessons from your trainer in order to teach your dog the basic exercises without the distraction of

If he's going to overcome his fears, your dog has to be exposed to many distractions, including other dogs.

other dogs. However, once your dog has learned the fundamentals, join a class so your dog is exposed to other dogs.

Your fearful dog will benefit from the class setting. If he's going to overcome his fears, he must be exposed to many distractions, including other dogs. He needs to learn that he can rely on you no matter what else is going on. The controlled environment of a training class may be the best place for that to happen. Besides, any good trainer will ensure that your dog is safe in class.

In a class setting, you'll learn a great deal about dog training as you watch other dog owners' mistakes and accomplishments. Your dog will also learn by watching the actions of well-adjusted, confident dogs.

Not all training classes are created equal, however. A trainer without enough knowledge or communication skills can actually make your dog worse rather than better. You may have to go to some effort to find the right training class to meet the needs of your dog.

Your task is made more difficult by the fact that no credentials are required to become an obedience instructor. No licensing process requires the trainer to have some level of expertise.

Checking the Yellow Pages or other advertising only demonstrates which trainer knows how to market well, not which trainer knows how to train a dog well. People who have barely taught their own dog basic obedience can teach classes. Pet superstores often run classes taught by clerks and advertise to prospective employees that no experience is necessary.

Finding a competent trainer can take a little digging, so start by asking some knowledgeable people which trainer they recommend. These are some good sources of information:

- **Your veterinarian.** Many veterinarians are knowledgeable about dog behavior and can recommend a good trainer. Although this can be an excellent source for referral, keep in mind that only a handful of veterinary schools in the nation offer any courses on animal behavior. Your veterinarian may be a fine surgeon and an excellent healthcare practitioner, but there is no guarantee that he or she is aware of dog-training activities in your community.

- **Your dog groomer.** If you go to a groomer, he or she may know about local dog trainers. Many groomers select the profession so they can pursue their multifaceted dog hobby. Again, not all dog groomers have all the information about trainers that you might want, but they can be a good place to start. (And remember, dog groomers are in a position to appreciate good basic training!)

- **Your boarding kennel.** If you board your dog when you're on vacation, the people who run your kennel may be able to suggest a trainer. Like dog groomers, many boarding kennel operators are informed about local dog activities, and they can be a good place to start looking for a trainer.

- **Your local animal shelter.** Some animal shelters and humane societies have lists of trainers in your area. If a trainer has worked successfully with problem dogs that have been adopted from the shelter, he or she may have the skills to work with your shy dog.

- **Your county extension office.** One of America's best-kept secrets is the wonderful Dog 4-H program operated by county extension offices throughout the nation. Even if you're not a potential 4-H member, local dog 4-H leaders may be able to recommend a trainer to you. (If you have a child who would like to train either your shy dog or another dog, approach your local 4-H program for this as well. Your child will learn positive lessons about dog care and training that will benefit him or her for a lifetime.)

- **Dog shows.** Hundreds of dog shows are held throughout the nation every year. Although most of the public attention focuses on the "beauty pageant" competition, almost every all-breed dog show also has an obedience trial going on simultaneously. Dogs in obedience competition are judged on their working performance, not on their looks. Find out when the next dog show will be held in your area, and go watch the obedience competition. The day will be well worth it; it's a pleasure to watch trained dogs perform.

See which dog-owner teams impress you (both in the ring and outside of it). Look for dogs that are working with their tails wagging and their heads held high. Look for handlers who give lots of praise and attention to their dogs—and a warm hug afterward, whether the dog passed the exercises or not. If you have a purebred dog, look for others of the same breed in competition.

Ask the people whose performances you admire where they get their training. Ask people with the same dog breed as yours where they go. People who compete in obedience competitions are the most knowledgeable group of people you can find. Talk to them about your problem dog, and find out which trainer they recommend. Make it clear you're looking for positive training methods.

CHECKING OUT THE TRAINER

Now that you've got a recommendation for a good trainer from a knowledgeable person, it's time to check out the trainer. Just because someone else had a good experience with the trainer doesn't mean you will. Some trainers have limitations: They may be great working with aggressive dogs, but not good at helping shy dogs. They may be wonderful Retriever trainers, but they might have no idea what to do with a shivering 3-pound dog who's too nervous to learn how to sit.

Ask Questions

Call and ask the trainer some questions. If you're calling a facility with more than one trainer, make sure you're getting responses from the person who will be teaching your class. Here are some issues to ask about:

1. Experience. What is the trainer's experience training timid dogs? Ask for specific examples of dogs who overcame their fearfulness. Ask for phone numbers of people with fearful dogs who were helped by the trainer.

2. Your breed. What is the trainer's experience with your breed of dog? With dogs of similar type?

3. Accomplishments. How long has the trainer been training dogs? How many of his or her own dogs has the trainer trained? What were the dogs' accomplishments? You may be just looking for basic training, but the more experience and accomplishments your trainer has achieved, the more likely he or she is to have addressed problems that may arise in training your dog.

4. Positive methods. What training methods does the trainer use? Look for someone who talks about positive reinforcement and motivating the dog to learn.

Take a Look for Yourself

The best way to evaluate a trainer is to watch him or her in action. Ask to sit in on a class. By the final week of a beginning obedience class, you should see the following:

- **Control.** The dogs are under good control. There's no barking in class. Dogs aren't jumping or lunging at each other (either in play or in aggression).

- **Basic concepts.** Most of the dogs are doing most of the basic commands most of the time. The dogs should understand the basic concepts of heel (walking at the owner's left side, sitting when the owner stops), stay (not moving from the designated spot until released by the owner), come (coming right to the owner), sit and down. After only a couple months of training, you can't expect the dogs to be perfect. However, you can expect the dogs to be under control and the owners to understand what the trainer is striving for.

- **Clarity.** The trainer's instructions should be clear and understandable. He or she should handle owners' questions in a constructive manner.

- **Fun.** The dogs and the owners should look like they're having fun. Dogs' tails should be wagging. Owners should be smiling at their dogs and giving them lots of praise. This should be the sort of place that both the dogs and their owners look forward to coming to each week.

- **Comfortable.** The class should feel comfortable to you. If it rubs you the wrong way, look for another instructor.

There is no place in dog training for abuse. Run—don't walk—out of class if you witness abuse. There is no excuse for hitting a dog, slapping him with a leash, kicking him or stringing him off the ground by his collar. If you see such practices or any treatment of an animal that you think is inappropriate, leave. The last thing your timid dog needs is abuse.

On the other extreme, just because trainers are using positive methods doesn't mean that the trainer knows anything about training a dog. If dogs are constantly being fed treats without receiving any information about what behavior is expected from them, the "training" is a waste of time, at best. Shy dogs crave structure and will find the canine free-for-all unsettling. This kind of atmosphere is likely to worsen your dog's problem.

Real dog training provides a structured, loving, supportive environment where dogs and their owners learn something.

If You Live in a Remote Area

People who live in rural areas may find it hard to locate the right trainer. If there's only one trainer in your community, you don't have the same set of choices available to dog lovers in an urban area. Still, observe some classes of the local trainer and see if you like his or her techniques. If it isn't good training, don't go. An alternative could be to have monthly private lessons at a trainer some distance from your home and then practice with friends in the intervening weeks. If you're persistent, you can find a way to get your instruction from someone who knows what he or she is doing. The expert direction of an excellent trainer is worth going the extra miles.

At this point, it may seem like too huge a task to find and evaluate the right trainer, but the effort will be more than worth it. Your trainer will be your partner in transforming your fearful dog into the great dog he can become. You'll be seeing a lot of this person in the upcoming months, so it's worth it to find the best.

When I first had Goldie, I went to a very poorly run class. During the first course, none of the dogs mastered even the most simple commands of stay, heel or come. We didn't try anything so advanced as down or stand. The small daughter of the trainer came to class with the trainer's Rottweiler, and this dog growled a number of times at other dogs and once defecated on the floor. These were not the signs of a successful trainer! My dog shivered in fear from day one and never relaxed.

When I went to the class of my next more experienced trainer, however, he placed Goldie and me next to an experienced fellow student with a calm, small dog. The first couple weeks of class, there were some barking and aggressive dogs. The trainer immediately dealt with those dogs and gave their owners the techniques for handling the disruptive behavior. By the end of the very first evening's class, Goldie was already beginning to shake less violently. All the dogs in the class made measurable progress during the 10-week class. That just goes to show that the right trainer can have a positive impact on a fearful dog's behavior.

STAY IN SCHOOL!

People drop out of training class at predictable times. Some drop out after the first night. I'm always stunned when people pay their money and never show up again. They must think training class is too overwhelming and that their dogs will never learn. Your dog can't benefit from class, however, if you don't take him.

People also often drop out after about a month. Some drop out because they seem to think they know how to train their dogs at this point. Others drop out because all the other dogs seem to be doing better than theirs and they feel like failures. The last few weeks of each class are the best, though. Your dog will learn, if you give him a chance. Just stick with it.

The more structured time you give your dog, the better he will learn. Don't be ashamed to repeat the beginners' class over and over until your dog starts to act comfortable and confident. You and your dog haven't flunked—you're just showing your dog how much you love him by giving him the extra time and attention he needs. The only way to fail is to give up on him and not provide him the opportunity to be the best he can be.

My own dog went through a beginners' class five times before she was promoted to the advanced class (or, as I like to call it, the talented and gifted class). I'm pretty sure five times through beginners is a Papillon record, since most Papillons are very quick learners (and because I was an experienced trainer).

When Goldie and I finally were promoted to the advanced class, I noticed that about half the advanced dogs were the sort of dogs you'd expect to see in the talented and gifted group—responsive, easy-to-train dogs that take naturally to obedience work. However, the other half of the class were dogs that had once been problem dogs—dog fighters, biters, shy dogs and dogs with a host of other problems. Working with their difficult dogs had become so important to these owners that training class became something more than 10 weeks of remedial education for their dogs: It had become an activity that the dog and owner enjoyed together over the course of years.

One dog owner interviewed for this book put it this way: "It's almost like my dog's greatest weakness became his greatest strength. You know how they show athletes in the Olympics who overcame childhood diseases and became super athletes as a result of the struggle? It's like that with my dog. He had to work so hard to get there that he has become a super-reliable competitor. His struggle has become his triumph."

With some patience from you, your dog will succeed. When you see that look of triumph in your dog's eyes, all the frustration of training a timid dog will be washed away by the joy in your heart.

So stay in school. Give your dog the time and consistent training he needs to succeed. He may surprise you beyond your wildest dreams.

Challenge: Quite a Challenge

Challenge went on to excel in obedience training and earned his Utility Dog title.

Barbara Griffin has accomplished feats in the world of competitive dog shows that most participants only achieve in their dreams. She has had 2 of the nation's top 10 obedience dogs—at the same time. She has had top winners in conformation. But of all the dogs she has trained and loved over her nearly 30 years of experience, one holds a special place in Barbara's heart: Challenge, a fearful Golden Retriever.

Barbara laughs at the irony of Challenge's name. Challenge's father, King, was ranked No. 7 out of all obedience dogs in the United States. "King was beginning to get older, so I decided to keep one of his puppies to take his place as my competition dog," she says. "Challenge's registered name was Gwinn-Dell's King's Challenge; he was supposed to carry on King's legacy. Instead, he was just a challenge!"

Crisis Strikes

Challenge was a normal, bright puppy—the pick of the litter. However, following his routine puppy shots at the age of 3 months, something went horribly wrong. The puppy had a reaction and became deathly ill. He ran a high fever and lapsed in and out of consciousness. After several days, the crisis passed and Challenge seemed to return to normal.

Barbara soon realized that the puppy wasn't as normal as he appeared. He never developed the size and heavy bone structure of other dogs of the same breeding. More importantly, he didn't have the same emotional stability. "I'd take him for a walk, and he'd watch kids playing with a ball," she says. "For the first couple of times the kids bounced the ball, he'd react like a typical Golden Retriever puppy, full of curiosity. Then at the third bounce, he'd hit the end of the leash like a rearing horse, suddenly terrified of the ball." Barbara adds that Challenge would see someone one time and approach the person with a happy Golden Retriever tail wag; the next time he'd see the same person, the dog would literally climb up a wall to get away.

Barbara explains, "The best guess we have is that the reaction to the shot created brain damage. His sudden, fearful reactions were like seizures. During these fear episodes, Challenge would physically change. A look of terror would come over his face. His eyes would look wild."

Barbara could have taken the advice of the several people who told her she ought to put Challenge to sleep. "People told me not to waste my time on a loser."

Instead, Barbara promised Challenge he would always have a loving home. She also promised him he'd earn his Utility Dog title, the elite level of obedience competition. Barbara recalls, "Everybody laughed at me when I told them that Challenge was my next Utility Dog."

A Big Breakthrough

Determined, Barbara began training Challenge. "After training two of the top obedience dogs in the country, it was quite a change," she says. "It was like going from driving a Porsche to driving a farm truck." She took Challenge to his first fun match (a practice dog show), where Barbara was accustomed to her dogs taking first place. Instead,

Challenge went running from the competition ring in terror when someone dropped an item near the ring.

"There were times it got very frustrating," Barbara reports. "It was like taking one step forward and six steps back."

Barbara's big breakthrough with Challenge came from a garbage can. She and the dog were walking past the garbage can when Challenge became terrified of the "killer" can. He bucked and reared, straining to run away. "I decided that, if it took the entire day, Challenge was going to get over his fear of that garbage can," Barbara says. "He was going to do a sit-stay right next to it, without fear. I took him as close to the can as he could go without fear, and we did a brief sit-stay. Then I brought him literally an inch closer and did a sit-stay. Over 45 minutes, we inched closer and closer, until finally he was calmly sitting next to the dreaded garbage can."

From this experience, Barbara learned the secret of training Challenge. "I couldn't tell him to stop being afraid—he couldn't understand that. But I could calmly, patiently, resolutely expect him to do his training exercises."

Becoming a Winner

Challenge did finally excel in obedience competition, and he earned his Utility Dog title. This meant that Challenge, the brain-damaged Golden Retriever, was (among other things) leaping over hurdles; performing stand, down, sit and come commands on hand signals; finding objects by scent; and allowing a judge to examine him minutely while Barbara stood silently 20 feet away across the ring—all in the midst of hundreds of other dogs at a show. Challenge earned four coveted Highest Scoring Dog in Trial awards.

"Those four High in Trials mean so much more to me than King's 33," says Barbara. "Challenge never liked competing that much. He did it just to please me."

Barbara recalls going to a dog-training seminar conducted by one of the nation's top competition trainers. The trainer explained it could take a lot of searching to find an outstanding obedience prospect. He said competitors may have to obtain and discard a number of dogs before the right one comes along. Barbara's voice, normally very matter-of-fact, betrays her emotion. "We should love and train the dogs we have, not just go out and find a different dog because it might be easier."

Barbara's experience with Challenge proves that any dog can become extraordinary. Challenge excelled not just as a competition dog, but also as a companion. "He was absolutely loyal, and an easy dog to live with," she says. "He was a fantastic guard dog, which was important to me because I traveled alone a lot back then. He was a very smart dog and was friendly with strangers when he wasn't protecting his property. He was a door-greeter and a tail-wagger. He was the perfect companion, and he slept by my bed at night."

"The bond I felt with Challenge was the strongest I've felt with any of my dogs," Barbara adds. "I think it's because I put so much of myself into him. There were times I cried in frustration: We had to work so hard to make any progress. But it was worth every minute of it. He was a great dog."

Love and hard work changed the "loser" dog that so many people said should be put to sleep. Challenge became a winner, both in the obedience ring and in Barbara's heart.

Chapter Five

Tips for Training a Shy Dog

Praise your dog and give her treats while she is in the stay position.

It's different training a shy dog than teaching a bold, easy-going dog. By their nature, fearful dogs are risk-averse. They are often so worried about doing the wrong thing that they are hard to coax into doing anything. This chapter underlines some of the most common problems faced by people who train nervous dogs. The following sections may reassure you that other dogs have faced exactly the same difficulties—and emerged as prize-winning competition dogs and wonderful family pets.

CREATING AN ATTITUDE

Figure out what makes your dog happy, and then do it. Make training sessions the happiest time of the day. Laugh with your dog, encourage her, let her know how proud you are of even the smallest accomplishment. Your shy dog will worry plenty about her mistakes; you don't need to. Concentrate on building your dog's confidence and pride whenever you're working together.

Rewards

Fearful dogs need lots of encouragement. Use food rewards, toys, play breaks, praise and anything else you can think of. It's vital that you provide plenty of positive rewards for your dog's work. Of course, this can be easier said than done.

Find a food reward your dog craves. Since many shy dogs are picky eaters, it can be hard to get your dog turned on to the fun of training. Try to pick a food reward that gets her excited: Even the most fearful dog may be able to overcome her nerves when bits of well-cooked liver or chicken are involved.

A few words of caution about food rewards: The reward you use should be basically healthy for the dog. The lower it is in salt, fat and sugar, the better. Don't overfeed with treats—no more than about 10 percent of a dog's diet should be anything other than her regular, balanced food. Also, be sure that the reward you choose is easy on your dog's digestive tract. The last thing you need is to cope with doggie diarrhea!

Many fearful dogs are also petting-averse. Your dog may find your pat on her head or stroke on her neck to be more an ordeal than a reward. Practice touching the dog regularly throughout the day. Give her treats and pet her. Help her become accustomed to the feel of your hand as a positive sensation. Many fearful dogs find strokes on the ears to be calming and soothing. Gently grasp the base of her ear with your thumb on the inside of the leather and your index finger on the outside. Gently stroke from the base to the tips of her ears. You're touching lots of acupressure points here, and most dogs find this sensation relaxing.

Many shy dogs also like to be scratched on the chest, and this is one petting reward that most dogs readily accept. Many also enjoy a scratch on the rump.

Play with your dog when she does well. When you release the dog from her exercise, clap your hands. Push gently at her chest. Scratch her back just above her tail. Bring her favorite toy and let her chase it or play tug of war with it. Let her know that training is a fun, happy time that both of you enjoy.

Don't forget to give plenty of vocal praise. Your dog will accept the happy sound of your voice with joy. "Good girl, I'm proud of you!" will mean more to her than any doggie treat. Praise should always accompany a food reward; it's never enough to just stick a doggie treat in her mouth. Tell her she's done well.

Repetition

All dogs need repetition in training, but your dog will need more of it. Because your dog is risk-averse, she needs to hear over and over from you that it's okay to take the step of completing the exercise. It's important that you practice the basic exercises every day.

It can be depressing when the person standing next to you in training class says, "I feel guilty, but we never practice," and then his or her dog works flawlessly. The reality is that your dog needs the extra repetition and won't work flawlessly without practice.

The good news is the repetition will quickly increase your dog's comfort level. For the first year of training with Goldie, we would practice first thing in the morning. That practice calmed her down and focused her for the rest of the day. On those rare occasions I was running late for work and didn't practice with her, I'd see a noticeable difference in her demeanor. She'd shake all day, seeming to have forgotten how to communicate with me. Although she took longer than other dogs to be confident enough to execute her commands in public, she obviously received benefit from just the activity of practicing. It was our daily morning practice that eventually conquered her constant shaking. Those practice sessions also ensured that her lessons were successful in the long run.

LEARNING TO SHAPE YOUR DOG'S BEHAVIOR

Shy dogs may be the hardest dogs to train. Bold, outgoing dogs will bounce around and show lots of behaviors; eventually, one of those behaviors will probably approximate the concept of the exercise you're working on. When you reward that behavior, the bold dog will do it again. Your shy dog is more likely to just stand there. You'll have to learn to use toys or treats to lure her into the position you want. Then be prepared to repeat that luring over and over—your risk-averse dog isn't likely to leap to any conclusions that she's supposed to actually move on her own. Your dog will learn little pieces of exercises, then eventually string those pieces together. It can be a slow process.

You might be tempted to speed up the process. That old-fashioned jerk-and-pull training may begin to seem like a good idea. Harsh training will only slow down your progress, though. When a fearful dog is jerked on the collar or shouted at, she's very likely to freeze and never want to move again.

Believe in your dog. With love and lots of encouragement, she can be trained.

Use a Clear Voice

Give verbal cues in a clear voice; don't make your dog guess whether she's supposed to do something. Clear, concise verbal cues spoken in a happy voice (not baby talk) will give your dog directions she can follow.

Expect Relapses

All dogs forget how to do their exercises at some point; it's apparently part of how dog brains store material. When dogs hit the rebellious ages of 12 months and 2 years, they will test the will of their owners. It's part of growing up. Even the best dogs will go through times when their performance isn't up to par.

Your fearful dog will have all the same regressions as every other dog. However, be prepared for the fact that your nervous dog may have a lot more of them. You'll be making great progress, then one day your dog will act as if she's never heard of the word "heel." Your dog will be bold and confident in class, until one day she'll start shaking with the same nerves she displayed six months ago. You'll be frustrated beyond belief.

Sometimes you can pinpoint what caused your dog's regression. Maybe the holidays are putting stress on the dog, or maybe your daily routines have changed. Just as often, you won't be able to begin to guess why your dog has regressed to her old, fearful ways.

Don't despair. Remind yourself that your dog has already overcome a lot and that somewhere in the back of her brain she knows the exercises. Just go back to training her in the exercises like you did the first time. Suddenly one day she'll start performing again, and she'll do it better than she did before.

Promise your dog infinite patience. Give her the time and support to work through her behavior regression and emerge more confident than ever before. Believe in your dog's ability to recover.

Go from Easy to Challenging Environments

It's easiest for your dog to learn an exercise in a quiet, familiar place. After she has conquered the lesson there, take her someplace more challenging. She may have to re-learn the exercise at that more challenging place, but be patient and teach it again. The general rule of thumb is this: Your dog can do more difficult things in an easy environment and less difficult things in a more demanding environment.

SOLVING TYPICAL TRAINING PROBLEMS

Three exercises generally pose special problems for shy dogs: stay, heel and come.

"Stay"

Your fearful dog may find it nerve-wracking when you walk away and expect her to stay in place. Just be patient. Start out standing directly in front of your dog on a sit-stay. Gradually increase the distance from the dog over time. Praise her and give her treats while she is in the stay position; this reinforces to her that she's making the right choice not to move.

"Heel"

Heeling is another typical problem command for a fearful dog. Your fearful dog probably wants to follow behind you, preferably with your body shielding her from people or other dogs. Techniques that may help your dog heel properly include holding treats in front of her nose, keeping such a brisk pace that your dog doesn't have time to think of anything else and keeping a happy commentary going so the dog thinks the two of you are on a great adventure. Generally, lagging will be a problem until your dog feels enough confidence to greet the world head-on by your side. Training techniques will hasten that day, but it's just going to take some time for your dog to feel that sense of security.

"Come"

Nervous dogs are afraid to come to someone who might be frightening to them. Never, ever call your dog over to you and then punish her, give her a bath or do anything else that is even mildly unpleasant. "Come" needs to be the best, most exciting thing that can happen to her. If she's reluctant to come, make it her idea. Run away from her so she's likely to follow, or hide in another room so that she has to find you. Whenever she comes, let her know you're proud and thrilled. Give her treats. Pet her in her favorite way. Let her know that she has accomplished something important.

Remember, shy and fearful dogs can learn every single thing that bold dogs can learn. Figure out what makes your dog respond, and reinforce that response over and over again. It will be worth it.

Tarah:
Adventures in Baby-Sitting

I really loved Tarah from the first time I saw her.

It all started for Peggy Gainer when she agreed to do some dog baby-sitting. "A friend of mine breeds beautiful Afghan Hounds," says Peggy. "A couple who'd bought one of her dogs three years before was divorcing and decided to return the dog to the breeder. My friend had a houseful of Afghans at the time and asked if I'd take care of this dog for two weeks so that she'd have time to integrate the dog into her household. I told her I'd be glad to help out, but I didn't want another dog."

When Peggy went to pick Tarah up at the airport, she couldn't believe the condition the dog was in. The dog's long,

75

silky hair was matted to the skin. She was severely underweight. And she was scared to death.

Love at First Sight

"I really loved Tarah from the first time I saw her," remembers Peggy, "but I couldn't imagine her fitting into our home. She didn't like my husband; in fact, she didn't like any men. And she was scared all the time." For the next two weeks, Peggy tried to make Tarah feel more comfortable. Nothing worked. The dog was in a state of constant terror and would run from the room every time she saw Peggy's husband. After two weeks, Peggy still couldn't imagine Tarah adjusting to her home. Because she was drawn to the dog, Peggy agreed to "baby-sit with an option to keep" Tarah, but she doubted that the dog could develop into a tolerable pet.

Peggy worked with Tarah every day, teaching her to sit and to accept being petted while she sat. She began taking Tarah to work with her and made sure every man who came through the door touched the dog. Soon Tarah wasn't running away from Peggy's husband. After a month, it became clear that Peggy's temporary baby-sitting agreement was going to turn into a full-time love affair with a dog of a lifetime.

"Tarah is different from other hounds," says Peggy. "I've never known an Afghan that will just hang around. She won't go more than 25 or 50 feet away from me, even if she's off the leash."

The Making of a Champion

Peggy had never thought about obedience training for Tarah until she went to the Afghan Hound Club of America national specialty show and saw an Afghan receive an obedience score of 199½ out of a possible 200 points. She thought that Tarah, with her submissive, loving personality, might become a competitive obedience dog.

"I'd only taken one obedience class with another dog before this," says Peggy. "That class used the old-fashioned pull-and-jerk method. Training through intimidation like that would have ruined Tarah." Peggy found a trainer who used positive training methods and helped build Tarah's confidence. "First we had to train her to have a confident attitude, then we trained her behavior," explains Peggy.

Still, training Tarah took endless patience. For two years, Tarah wouldn't come when she was called unless she was on a leash. Finally,

Peggy began to hide and then call Tarah. Peggy says with a laugh, "Suddenly Tarah said, 'Golly, where's Mom?' and began to look for me."

After four years of classes, Tarah was ready to compete for her Companion Dog title. Tarah excelled. In 1994, she was rated as the top obedience Afghan Hound in the country. She has other accomplishments, as well: Her speed and hunting instincts have earned her the title of Field Champion in lure coursing events, and she's a Canine Good Citizen.

But the titles and awards are just icing on the cake. "What's most important is that Tarah is my best friend," Peggy says. "Tarah knows what I'm thinking and feeling; we can read each other like books. I've never had a relationship like this. She lies on my bed with me if I'm sick. Other Afghans will go running off as soon as you take off their leashes; Tarah stays with me, asking me what I want of her."

Little Pleasures Mean a Lot

Since living with and training Tarah, Peggy has learned that people who train shy dogs have to get out of themselves and into their dogs—and learn more empathy as a result. "People say that you shouldn't sweat the small things, but Tarah taught me that the small things make a difference," Peggy says. " To learn to read Tarah, I had to watch for the subtleties. I also learned to watch people more carefully from this experience. I understand my husband and my friends better, because I've learned to look for what they're telling me without words."

To an observer, this graceful dog with the luminous eyes shows no sign of shyness. However, some things can still trigger a fearful response. "Tarah can't stand yelling," says Peggy. "Recently I scolded my young dog for misbehaving, and poor Tarah pooped on the floor. I realized that I had made a mistake when I raised my voice in her presence. It's important for people with shy dogs to remember that the dogs don't behave this way on purpose. They don't want to pee on the floor when they get scared. There's something you've done, or something that you've allowed to happen, that triggers the behavior."

Today, Tarah looks far younger than her 10 years. She still comes to obedience class and obviously relishes retrieving her dumbbell and leaping over jumps. But mostly I notice the relationship between Tarah and Peggy. The dog's large, sweet eyes are always on the woman she obviously adores. Then Peggy smiles, gives Tarah a huge hug and says, "I just love this dog!"

Chapter Six

More of the Real World

Your dog could become date bait!

Once you've begun to conquer training class, your dog is ready to begin living life as a normal, social pet. It's time to expose him to more of the real world. Now that he has become familiar with his neighborhood, has relaxed at some quiet parks and has been to school, he's ready for a rich variety of experiences. His education isn't complete without being exposed to the noisier side of life. It's time to teach your dog to accept—or at least tolerate—the touch of strangers.

THE BRIBERY METHOD

One way to teach your dog to make friends is to bribe him. Have the person greeting your dog give your dog a treat. The tidbit can't be just a chunk of dry kibble—yuck. Don't try to be coy and use a super-healthy doggie treat that's really just a kibble shaped like a bone. The tidbit should be something moist and juicy—preferably with the foul smell that dogs love. Try well-boiled liver, or commercial hot dogs designed for babies (they're at least marginally healthier than hot dogs sold to adults.)

With great exaggeration and ceremony, give the delicious, smelly, moist tidbit to your friend. Make sure the dog sees you giving your friend the food. Your dog needs to know that your friend has the best tidbit of all time in his or her possession. Your friend should reach out his or her hand with the treat and encourage your dog to come eat the tidbit.

When your friend offers your dog the treat, you should stay absolutely quiet. You may think if you encourage your dog to talk to strangers, he'll feel more secure. Not so. The timid dog interprets your talking as something that bonds the two of you together. This exercise teaches the dog to begin to develop relationships with other humans in addition to you. By remaining silent and motionless—even look away from your dog—it becomes clear to the dog that he can accept the tempting tidbit on his own.

Some dogs won't take even the most tempting treat from people they don't know. If your dog refuses the food at first, it may help to have your friend turn sideways, which is a less threatening posture for the dog. Also have your friend look away from the dog, since direct eye contact from a person he doesn't know may intimidate your shy dog. Keep giving your dog opportunities to eat delicious tidbits offered by your friends. Sooner or later, almost every dog will learn to accept food from non-threatening people.

Continue this technique regularly with friends. Graduate to friendly strangers you meet when you're walking your dog. Everyone always wants to pet your dog, right? You're probably sick of saying, "I'm sorry, my dog is too shy." This is the chance to see if the person who wants to pet your dog is a real dog lover. Hand him or her a morsel of a doggie treat and tell him or her to give it to your dog. A true dog lover will feel honored.

Many fearful dogs soon become people-friendly. Why not, when nearly everyone they meet seems to carry some wonderful, smelly, gooey dog treat? Even if your dog doesn't become outgoing toward people with this technique, he'll probably stop shrinking away from them. He'll begin to look directly at people in order to size up their potential as carriers of baby hot dogs. The look of fear and suspicion on your dog's face will be replaced by greed—he'll look like a regular dog!

Prolonging the Exposure

After your dog is taking treats from strangers, prolong the interaction. Ask the person holding the doggie treat to grasp the treat firmly in his or her hand and to make the dog work to eat it. When your dog has become comfortable wrestling the tidbit out of a hand, ask the person to gently scratch the dog's chest. Over time, the dog will associate a stranger's outstretched hand and petting with food. Eventually, many timid dogs learn to enjoy the touch of strangers.

Petting During a Sit-Stay or Stand-Stay

As your dog loses his dread of strangers and also becomes competent at his training exercises, it's time to have strangers touch the dog while the dog is performing a sit-stay or stand-stay. Put your dog in a sit-stay and ask a stranger to gently pet him. Keep the dog in his sit-stay; he's got to learn to stay still and accept the attention. His nervousness will be diverted by the concentration it takes to do the task.

As always, it's your primary responsibility to protect your dog. Be sure the stranger isn't putting too much pressure on the dog. It's amazing what strangers will do with a dog they've never seen before. If you have a small dog, the person might try to pick him up, or might reach down to hug your dog. Small children will see what places their fingers fit. Don't let anyone touch your dog inappropriately. Don't let a stranger reprimand your dog or speak to him in a harsh voice. Give clear instructions for light, gentle touching, and end the session if anyone doesn't follow your instructions.

In training class, your dog will learn the "Stand for Examination" exercise, in which the dog must stand motionless while a stranger touches him. When your dog becomes steady in this exercise, it's great practice to have friends and acquaintances examine the dog. If you teach your dog to stand for examination and accept touching from a variety of people, within a few weeks your dog will be much more tolerant of touch in any situation that might come up.

Being petted by strangers while doing a sit-stay or stand-stay isn't as much fun for your dog as the bribery method of dog interaction. However, it does teach your dog to react calmly no matter what person approaches him. This will make trips to the veterinarian much less traumatic, and it will reduce his flight or fight response. Using both the bribery method and the sit-stay or stand-stay exercise will greatly reduce your dog's dread of strangers. He may even become something of a party animal!

DOGGIE DIVERSITY

Make sure your dog meets the widest possible cross-section of people. Introduce your dog to men and women, children and adults. Be sure to introduce your dog to people of different ethnic groups and national origins. Dogs are observant and can be wary of people who have different skin color than their owner. Let him hear the tones and cadences of foreign languages; he may not like it at first when people sound different to him. Expose the dog to people in wheelchairs and walkers. Shy dogs also often fear people of the opposite sex from their owner. Give your dog a chance to learn to be tolerant of all people, not just people who look and sound exactly like you do.

CHALLENGING PLACES

Now your dog is ready to start going to more challenging places. Take him into the city and walk him on busy sidewalks. Take him to the shopping mall and practice his training exercises while dozens of people walk by. (Ignore their comments about how they wish their children were as well-behaved as your dog.) Take him to a pet superstore and practice his training while all the other dogs are jumping all over the place and urinating on the fixtures. Take your dog to a fun match (a practice dog show); sit together and watch the other dogs compete. Take your dog to an agility competition and watch him watch the other dogs jump and run. You'll both enjoy the excitement. Take him to your family parties and your friends' barbecues—he'll be so well-behaved at this point that he'll be welcome everywhere.

The more places your dog goes, and the more sights he sees and noises he hears, the better off he'll be. He may be nervous at first, but if you stick with this practice, he'll learn to tolerate these environments. One day you'll realize he's wagging his tail as soon as he's out of the car, looking forward to his next adventure.

The time that it took to train your dog and desensitize him will be worth it. The two of you will have a great time going places together. All this effort will get you out of the house and exploring your community more, too. That's a good thing. When you take your dog on his adventures, take your spouse and the kids with you, too. You'll all have a bonding experience.

(There's an ancillary advantage to all of this for single dog owners. People of the opposite sex who would never approach you alone will be glad to help out by petting your dog or feeding him tidbits. Your dog could become date bait! Who knows? The dog lover who's willing to feed your dog some slimy treat could be your soul mate. Just think how much our dogs can do for us.)

Get the dog out the front door, and both of you go have some fun!

Colter: The Renaissance Dog

Jessica Martin, age 7, and Colter, a 9-year-old Sheltie, earned a blue ribbon together in Agility.

Colter nudges his elegant head into owner Bob Lackey's hand. "Colter is a Renaissance dog," says Bob while he pets the quiet Shetland Sheepdog. "He's been successful at everything he's tried."

Colter has racked up an impressive list of accomplishments. He has a Companion Dog obedience title from the American Kennel Club. He demonstrated his athleticism and partnership with Bob when he earned a novice agility title with the North American Dog Agility Council. He's an official AKC Canine Good Citizen. As a 9-year-old, he passed a herding instinct test with flying colors. Colter is also a certified therapy dog and a frequent visitor to nursing homes. In fact, there are few areas of dog activity in which Colter hasn't demonstrated proficiency.

It didn't start out this way.

85

Scared from the Start

"When we chose Colter, we didn't know a lot about dogs," Bob admits. "In retrospect, we realize he was very timid from the time we brought him home as an 8-week-old puppy."

Colter's natural reaction to anything that frightened him was to run, in a state of panic, for a secure area. He was very sensitive to noise and would bolt away from any loud or unfamiliar sound. He was afraid of any new environment and would try to run out of strange buildings. If it rained outside, he'd bark at the rain.

When Colter was 6 months old, Bob and his wife Lana took the dog to his first training class. That's when they noticed there was something very different about their dog. "Colter was shaking like it was 20 degrees below zero," Bob remembers. "He was crouched under a chair while the other dogs were jumping around trying to play. His fear decreased very little during the eight weeks of class. And while Colter was shaking with fear, I noticed that everybody else's dog was apparently having a good time." Although Colter was learning the training exercises, he was too fearful to successfully execute them in class.

When Colter was 2 years old, Bob and Lana tried a second class with a different trainer. Colter was again unable to conquer his nervousness in class.

Getting Motivated

Finally, when Colter was 4, they took him to a third training class. This time they made some measurable progress. "Our trainer teaches classes four nights a week," says Bob. "I'd take Colter to our regular class each Thursday, then Colter and I would practice in the corner during the other three nights' classes." Eventually, working with all these strange dogs in the background, Colter learned to do his training exercises no matter what else was happening. He stopped shaking and eventually learned to have fun in class.

"We also learned that food is a motivator and to emphasize the positive aspects of training," Bob adds. "We do lots of praise and play with the dog when he's done it right. That was very important to Colter. He's very motivated by food and positive reinforcement."

After finding the right trainer and techniques for Colter, Bob and Lana stuck with the dog's training. They still practice their training routines several nights a week, and they still attend classes with the same trainer.

Bob remembers going to an obedience competition to watch other dogs when Colter was 4 years old. "There was a Sheltie in the ring who had done very well. I walked up to the dog's owner and congratulated him on his dog's fine performance. I said, 'I wish my dog could do that.' The man said that Colter *could* do it. I told him, 'The chance of that is zero.'" Not only did Colter eventually earn his obedience title, but he's still used in obedience and agility demonstrations at the age of 9½.

Having the Time of His Life

Bob and Lana are quick to say that Colter is not always quiet and shy. He's protective of the house. He also proved to be a happy maniac when given a herding instinct test. "He was having so much fun that he wouldn't come back to me when I called him—and Colter always comes when he's called," Bob says with a laugh. "I finally had to pick him up and carry him out. As I was carrying him, Colter's legs were running through the air like a cartoon dog, trying to get back to the herding test. He was having the time of his life."

Colter is also a therapy dog. Therapy dogs go into nursing homes, retirement facilities, hospitals, hospices and other places where people have limited opportunities to interact with the larger community. Colter is certified with two national sponsoring organizations: Therapy Dog International and Therapy Dogs, Inc.

How does Bob and Lana's shy dog do in the demanding environment of a nursing home? "Colter's reserved nature works well in his nursing home visits," Bob says. "Many of the nursing home residents whom we see are physically frail. They are sometimes a little nervous around a boisterous, outgoing dog. Colter is very gentle and quiet. He'll stand patiently while the nursing home residents pet him. Colter is a Sheltie and looks a lot like a Collie. Many of the residents had Collies when they were younger, and they all know Lassie. Colter's presence gives them a chance to reminisce about those dogs and other events in their lives."

Good Advice

What advice does Bob have for people who are considering adopting or purchasing a timid dog? "I'd give the same advice to someone considering a timid dog as I would to a person considering purchasing or adopting any dog," he says. "Think about what you're getting a dog for. I see people all the time with Border Collies or Australian Shepherds who apparently thought these active, working dogs would turn out to be quiet indoor pets. They selected the wrong dog for their needs. If you want to compete and get the top scores in agility or obedience competition, get a more assertive, outgoing dog—possibly a dog bred for work. But if you want a quiet companion, a more timid dog can be a good choice. If you get a fearful dog, you'll have to work and work and work to make progress. It's essential to find a good trainer to work with, one who will tailor a training program to your dog's special needs. But your progress is sweeter when you succeed."

Was there an age at which Colter stopped making progress? Bob answers, "Colter's basic problem has never gone away. He's innately shy. What Colter has learned to do is compensate for his shyness. He learns new ways to compensate, so his behavior gets calmer all the time. That process of compensation has continued throughout his life."

Colter moves from nuzzling Bob to looking for some attention from Lana. He offers to shake hands, something he recently learned. Lana gives him a treat for his efforts. Colter, the Renaissance dog who can do it all, contentedly rests between his owners, waiting patiently for his next adventure.

Chapter Seven

Phobias

Some object or situation likely will send your dog into an uncontrollable, irrational panic.

Most nervous dogs have phobias. Some object or situation probably will send your dog into an uncontrollable, irrational panic. It might be the vacuum cleaner, a noisy fan or a brick wall, but your dog is convinced the object has the power to kill her. She can quickly become dangerous to herself or others; it's likely that she'll run away from the object of her fear—possibly into the path of an oncoming car. If she's a fear-biter, she may respond to your efforts to control her with a nasty bite.

Sometimes you'll know the cause of your dog's phobia, and sometimes you won't. A single, specific traumatic incident can trigger a phobia. For instance, let's say a child was given the chore of vacuuming the house and the family dog started barking at the vacuum. The child decided to "play" with the barking dog by chasing her with the vacuum. Within moments, the dog was in a panic, terrified of the vacuum. The dog never forgot the experience and developed a phobia of vacuums, which made regular housecleaning chores around the house a misery for everyone.

It isn't always so easy to pinpoint the cause of a phobia, though. A dog owner I interviewed has a dog who's terrified of mailboxes. "When we go on a walk and she sees one of the big blue mailboxes on a street corner, she absolutely panics," the owner reports. "I've had this dog since she was a puppy, and I'm quite sure she's never had a bad experience with a mailbox. One has never jumped out and grabbed her. I have no idea why she decided to become terrified of mailboxes."

Dealing with a phobia requires desensitizing the dog to the object of her fear. She must become used to the object and learn to cope with it, if not ignore it. It's a gradual process that may take weeks or even months to successfully complete. The results can be worth the patience, however, and bring about an improved quality of life for both you and your dog.

The following techniques can help your dog overcome her phobias:

1. Turn scary objects into food dispensers. One fine trainer I know had a Border Collie who was terrified of the machines that dispense soft drink cans. Not only do these machines periodically make loud humming sounds, but they also make crashing, metallic noises when the cans come out. This trainer put a little food reward in the can dispenser and let her dog find the food. Then she taught her dog to paw at the soda can selection buttons; when the dog did so, food would "magically" appear in the can dispenser. Soon this dog learned to love soda machines and would press the buttons to earn his food reward.

Nellie's fear of leashes is being eased using this technique. Jean began by placing treats near Nellie's leash and requiring the dog to come close to the leash in order to get the treat. Once Nellie became desensitized to the leash enough to pick up a treat next to the leash, Jean left the treat snarled inside the leash. Nellie had to unsnarl the leash to find the treat, further desensitizing her to the object of her fear. Nellie is still nervous when a leash drags behind her, but she is slowly learning to associate a leash with treats.

2. Focus your dog on a training exercise. Distracting your dog with training exercises can help her deal with a phobia.

Barbara Griffin used this approach to desensitize Challenge to a garbage can. Barbara put Challenge in a sit-stay as close to the dreaded garbage can as she could get him. After he was calmly doing his sit-stay, she brought him an inch closer and then did another sit-stay. It took 45 minutes, but finally Challenge sat right next to the garbage can and was able to calmly execute his sit-stay.

If your dog finds a place intimidating, try Barbara's sit-stay technique, or try heeling your dog at a brisk pace near the object of her fear. Your dog will be busy concentrating on the task at hand and will stop fixating on her phobia.

This technique is used by humans all the time. One of my brothers was on a state championship high school football team. He still remembers being scared when he looked at players across the line. He said to me, "If you're well-drilled in football, you know the routine: blasting off with your left foot, right foot, boom—your forearm comes up. Even if the guy across the line scares the heck out of you, if you hear 'hut two, hut,' you blast off on the second hut. The muscle memory makes you do it, and you completely forget your fear." Think of Olympic figure skaters who explain that they are terrified until they hear their music and calmly do their routine. By giving your dog her training exercises to focus on, she'll be able to focus on what she knows instead of focusing on her fears.

3. Play a desensitization tape. Exposure at low levels can help overcome a noise phobia. For example, many dogs are terrified of the sound of thunder. Owners play high-quality commercial recordings of thunder storms softly in the background while playing games with their dogs or giving them treats. Over time, increase the volume until the dog ignores the sound of thunder and thinks about the play time and the treats.

4. Give your dog a reassurance word. Give your dog a consistent word that lets her know that you're aware of whatever concerns her but that there's nothing to be afraid of. Living downtown in a sizable city, I had problems with Goldie's fear of loud noises. I never noticed all the noises on my street until I had a dog who trembled at the morning garbage truck pickup, who dove for cover when helicopters on the way to the nearby hospital flew overhead, who cringed at the sounds of sirens and who cowered at the noises of revelers in the streets. Before I had Goldie, I'd thought my city neighborhood was relatively quiet!

Each time there was a startling noise, I'd say, "It's just a noise" in a matter-of-fact tone of voice. Now, when Goldie hears a loud noise, she looks over at me. I say, "It's just a noise," and she relaxes. When I acknowledge the noise and then reassure Goldie that there's nothing to fear, Goldie knows that her pack leader (me) is aware of the situation and has it under control. She can relax and follow the pack leader.

Goldie now routinely walks directly next to buses with their engines running, hops over vacuum hoses of commercial cleaning vehicles and enjoys noisy city life without fear. That success is a combination of regular exposure to the stimulus and matter-of-fact reassurance from me that she's in no danger.

5. Expose your dog. Give your dog constant, gradually escalating exposure to the object of her fear. It's common for a dog to be afraid of noisy household items such as vacuum cleaners (even without the experience of one chasing her through the house) or fans. If your dog fears the vacuum, leave it out in a room for a few days. Eventually, the dog will get used to its presence. After the dog is calm in its presence, run the vacuum cleaner in another room while you play with the dog or practice her training exercises on the other side of the house. When your dog is relaxed with that (which may take several sessions over the course of a few weeks), bring the vacuum closer. Continue gradually desensitizing the dog by bringing the vacuum closer and closer, until finally you can operate the vacuum in the same room with a calm dog.

6. Be matter-of-fact. Remember to speak to the dog in a matter-of-fact tone of voice. Baby talk makes the situation worse. Don't coo, "Poor Princess, please don't be afraid of the big, mean garbage can." To a dog, a baby talk tone is the equivalent of a whine. (By now, you've surely stopped whining!) When you speak baby talk to your dog, you're communicating that she has reason to be afraid.

On the other hand, don't be impatient or harsh. Don't lose your temper, even though your dog's irrational phobia can be frustrating. Your dog's fear is real to her, and your angry tone will only add to her fear. A calm, patient, matter-of-fact voice is an important tool in helping your dog recover from her fear.

7. Ignore it. At times it's wisest to ignore the phobia. The phobias described here needed to be dealt with: Jean's dog needed to be secure on her leash. All dogs encounter garbage cans and vacuum cleaners. My city dog had to get used to her noisy environment. However, if your dog is terrified of an object that she's unlikely to ever encounter again, it's okay to move on and forget it. Not every moment of every day has to be an object lesson.

PHOBIAS CREATED BY ABUSE

Some dogs have phobias created by abuse. Dogs who have been beaten are afraid if you raise your hand near them. Dogs who have been tied up for long periods of time can panic when they're tied up again. Dogs who lived in unclean cages can be terrified of kennels.

Breaking these phobias will unhappily bring back frightening memories to your dog. Think about whether your dog really needs to overcome the phobia, or whether you can create an environment in which the dog isn't exposed to the object of her phobia. If you can avoid the exposure, do it. Your abused dog deserves a break.

However, if the dog needs to be desensitized to a phobia created by abuse, do it in small steps. If she's afraid of certain arm movements, have a favorite treat or toy in your hand. Move your arm in a variety of ways, playing with your dog, giving her treats and praising her. Every once in a while, raise your arm in the manner she finds frightening for just a fraction of a second, and continue the game. Over time, she'll associate lots of weird arm movements with her seemingly odd but kind new owner, and she will disassociate the arm movements with abuse. The key is to be gradual and playful.

Dogs who were kept isolated in cages for prolonged periods of time—especially in filthy conditions—may fear crates. Since use of a crate is important for transporting your dog and for other humane purposes, use gradual deconditioning to overcome the problem. Start out with a crate placed in plain sight. Give the dog treats near the crate. Over time, put the dog's favorite treats in the crate. Begin to feed the dog in the crate. Slowly let the dog learn that her clean crate with the soft bedding is a very different place than the location of her abuse.

Remember not to add to the dog's feelings of insecurity by either talking in baby talk or by being harsh. While being sensitive to your dog's background, concentrate patiently on the task at hand rather than a constant replay of her past life.

Don't, under any circumstances, decide that a dog with a past history of abuse should "just do it." Using the example of the crate, it's unrealistic and cruel to put the abused dog into the crate and expect her to eventually just get over her fear. We wouldn't help an ex-prisoner of war by confining him in a small cell and telling him to just deal with his claustrophobia. A dog remembers her abuse just as vividly and needs to be gently and unemotionally guided to an understanding that not all cages are dangerous, that not all raised arms mean pain and that not all collars are instruments of torture. Moving too quickly will make that lesson impossible to learn.

Be consistent and gently determined in overcoming your dog's phobias. It can be painful and frustrating, but it's important to your dog's quality of life to help her through these fears. Conquering her fears will bring the two of you closer together.

Reno: Too Much to Handle?

Reno, pictured with owner Chris Primmer, has become mad about his tennis balls.

Chris Primmer can't remember a time when she hasn't trained dogs. Her dogs have earned an impressive array of obedience and agility titles. A year and a half ago, however, everyone thought Chris had taken on too much when she rescued her German Shepherd Dog, Reno. Her husband, Jim, a respected dog trainer in his own right, said to her, "This time you've bitten off more than you can chew. This is one dog even you can't save."

Chris adopted Reno when he was 2½ years old. Before coming to Chris, Reno had been owned by a woman who was widowed and had purchased the dog for protection for herself and her five young boys. Unfortunately, the woman became afraid of Reno.

Assessing the Damage

When Chris adopted Reno, he was in bad physical condition. "He was emaciated," Chris recalls. "He had more worms than Carter's got pills. He was extremely uncoordinated. He had injured his thigh at some

97

point, and the wound didn't heal properly, so the muscles in his thigh had atrophied."

That wasn't the worst of it, either: "His eyes were dead," Chris says. "There was no life in his eyes." But Chris felt a strong attraction to Reno from the very beginning. "Reno was the first dog that I've rescued that bonded like glue from the very first day."

Worse than Reno's physical problems were his behavior problems. "He had no manners. But when I'd try to discipline him, he'd hit the ground in terror," says Chris. "I've always played with my dogs by blowing in their faces. When I blew in Reno's face, he freaked out. We were in a motel room and he tried to get under the bed. He started ramming his head into a wooden board on the side of the bed. It was awful."

When people other than Chris tried to pet Reno, he would cringe with his head to the ground and his tail tucked between his legs. He was especially afraid of men. Reno's fear response could sometimes take the form of aggression. He had the traits of a fear-biter: He had nipped at the boys who had lived with him in his original home, and there were reports that he had acted aggressively toward men.

The dog was also a runner. With no training, Reno put Chris to the test when he got out of her grasp. "He wears a collar 24 hours a day now," Chris explains. "I needed something to grab onto."

Stepping Stones

Chris's first step was to begin Reno's physical rehabilitation. She cut his long nails, gave him regular baths and fed him top-quality dog food. Reno also got plenty of opportunities for healthy exercise to help his atrophied thigh gain muscle mass.

The next priority was teaching the dog to play. "By the time I had Reno six months, he'd begun to figure out the concept of play," Chris says. "I started out tossing him popcorn, since both of us like it. The game is that he has to catch it in the air."

Once Reno mastered the popcorn, he began to play fetch with a tennis ball. "Now he'll play with a tennis ball for hours—he's also learned to play with other dogs," Chris says. "Reno became a much better, more mellow pet after he learned to play."

Chris enrolled Reno in training class as soon as she got him. "Reno came from a place where he got little attention and absolutely no discipline. Our home is a highly structured environment for the dogs. He needed training to understand our structure. He learned he could depend on me to be consistent. The most important thing for Reno is consistency. I learned that, with honest rules, he'll follow me to the ends of the earth."

Much of Chris's week involves dog activities: teaching agility, attending obedience class and going to dog performance events. For the first year she had Reno, she brought the dog with her every place she went. He was exposed to hundreds of other dogs in dozens of settings. "We put socialization into high gear," she reports. "I took him everywhere with me. I asked everyone to give him treats, so he saw strangers as something friendly instead of something to fear."

Chris is the first to admit that she made some mistakes with Reno, though. "When Reno became possessive of his space, I told him he was a good boy. Then one day a friend came up to hug me at agility school. Out of the corner of my eye I saw Reno begin to jump from his exercise pen. Fortunately, I was able to stop him before anything happened. I learned from that experience that I have to be careful of his protective tendencies. He would bite anyone—including my husband, Jim— if he thought I was in danger."

A Lesson in Life

Chris smiles with pride at the progress Reno has made in the year and a half that she's had him. "His obedience is really coming along. I was practicing with Reno before class recently, and the trainer said, 'That dog works for you. His heart shows through his eyes.'

"It's fun to go to dog shows and see people who haven't seen Reno since I first got him," she says. "There's life in his eyes. His ears are forward and his posture is friendly. People don't believe he's the same dog."

Still, Chris points out that after only a year and a half, Reno is very much a work in progress. She can't always trust him not to go running off when he has the chance. She's still working on the boundaries of his protectiveness, encouraging appropriate behavior and discouraging overprotectiveness. She knows he has many more months of work before he can hope to compete for an obedience title. But Chris also acknowledges that the dog has come a long way.

Was it worth putting all this work into Reno? "This dog loves unconditionally," says Chris with emotion. "He has reminded me that there's still hope for dogs like him. So many people told me that this time I couldn't do it. They told me I couldn't save him. But with consistent boundaries and rules, he's made it. That's a good lesson in life."

Chapter Eight

The Worst Behaviors: Uncontrolled Urination, Nervous Defecation and Fear-Biting

Your dog isn't doing this behavior on purpose.

Some problems just seem overwhelming. Countless dogs are euthanized every year because their owners couldn't cope with their dogs' worst behaviors. Among the most common problems that lead to a return to the breeder, a return to the animal shelter or a one-way visit to the veterinarian's office are submissive urination, nervous defecation and fear-biting. With some hard work and dedication, you can solve these problems.

SUBMISSIVE URINATION

Your fantasy is to come home from a hard day's work and be greeted at your door by your loving dog. Well, Fido greets you, all right. He wriggles at your feet, turns on his back, averts his eyes from your face and wets the floor. Welcome home.

This behavior is classic submissive urination. This is how the lowest-ranking dogs in the pack demonstrate their submission to the more dominant dogs. When he shows his belly and urinates, your dog is signaling to you that he is extremely submissive to you, and he's reassuring you that he's not a threat to your dominant role in the household. He can be a perfectly housebroken dog and still submissively urinate.

Why do some dogs have an innate urge to urinate to show their deference to dogs (or to humans) they perceive as dominant? I don't have a clue. I've just decided that it's the canine equivalent of the person who says, "I was so nervous, I felt like I was going to pee in my pants." Unfortunately, your dog is peeing on your pants—and on your carpet.

Your natural reaction is probably to express dismay or perhaps disgust. Even a kind person can lose his or her temper and yell at the dog. Of course, angry reactions make the problem worse. Your dog's submissive urination is an instinctive reaction to express his submission. The more he's punished, the worse the problem will get.

Building your dog's confidence is the key to ending submissive urination. A more confident dog doesn't need to show this form of extreme submission. The steps outlined in this book—particularly training and exposing your dog to a variety of situations—will in all likelihood cure the problem.

Meanwhile, you can help speed up the cure by taking these steps.

How to Stop Submission Urination

1. Stop head-petting. Don't pet your dog on the top of his head. Reaching above a dog's head is very dominant behavior from a dog's point of view. One person reported a dog who was completely cured of a submissive urination habit when everyone started scratching the dog on her chin or chest instead of patting her on the head.

2. Speak in a gentle voice. Don't use baby talk, but be sure your voice isn't brusque or gruff. Have your friends and family listen to you. A gruff or sharp voice can sound like a bark to a dog, triggering his submissive pack instincts.

3. Don't be emotional. Never show an emotional reaction to your dog's submissive urination. Don't scold, don't lament and don't try to comfort him. Ignore the behavior. Anticipate the times when submissive urination is likely to occur, and plan accordingly. For example, many fearful dogs will submissively urinate when their owners come home. To end or at least minimize the urination behavior, try to make your homecomings matter-of-fact. Don't throw open the door and fuss all over your dog—it will overwhelm him. Instead, give him a quiet, subdued greeting. You might try giving him no greeting at all for a few minutes, then greeting him quietly. If you're not distraught with emotion, your dog also is less likely to be distraught with emotion.

If you know an action is likely to create submissive urination, do it someplace other than on your heirloom Persian rug. If your dog usually urinates when he greets you, say hello in the kitchen rather than in the living room.

Some effective enzyme-based products on the market eliminate the odors of urine and feces from your carpet. Use them to lessen the impact on your carpet and flooring.

4. Expect it. Expect submissive urination during training, especially at class. As before, don't reprimand your dog. He isn't doing this behavior on purpose. If he urinates while you are practicing an exercise, ignore the behavior. Calmly move over and continue the exercise several feet away from the puddle. When you're finished with the exercise, mop up the puddle.

It's very important to complete the training exercise before wiping up the puddle. If you stop the training and mop up, your dog learns that he can stop the training (which is stretching his comfort level at the moment) by urinating. This seems like a good deal to him! If the urination has absolutely no effect, the behavior will end—usually in the course of just a few weeks.

5. Potty the dog. Make sure you potty the dog well before taking him into a situation in which submissive urination is likely. This may reduce his urge to urinate—and it will also reduce the size of the mess you have to deal with.

NERVOUS DEFECATION

Nervous defecation is similar to submissive urination: It's some dogs' physiological response to fear. Your dog can be perfectly housebroken but unable to stop his nervous defecation.

This habit usually is triggered by events that "frighten the stuffing" out of your dog. Many anxious dogs defecate when they're riding in a car, in training class or going to a crowded mall parking lot. As with submissive urination, scolding the dog just makes his problem worse.

Try these techniques to help manage the problem until your dog's increasing confidence solves the problem.

How to Stop Nervous Defecation

1. Use suppositories. Clean out your dog's bowels before subjecting him to a situation that's likely to cause nervous defecation. Many long-time breeders and trainers recommend inserting the tip of a long kitchen match into the dog's rectum to act as a suppository. Veterinarians recommend using a baby glycerin suppository.

I know, you can't imagine doing such a thing—but look at the alternatives, and it doesn't seem to be such a bad idea. You don't want your dog defecating in the car. If he's confined to a crate, his excrement will get all over him. This is always ugly, and particularly horrible with a long-haired breed. If your dog isn't confined to a crate, goodness knows where the excrement will end up. In any event, your car will never smell the same. If your dog makes it through the car ride, then he's going to defecate in front of your training class, your friends or a crowd. Given your choices, using a suppository on your dog isn't such a bad idea, is it? (I didn't say the solution was pleasant; I just said it would help solve the problem!)

2. Keep going. As with submissive urination, don't stop what you're doing (such as a training exercise) just because your dog defecated. You'll be reinforcing that the best way out of a situation that stretches his comfort zone is to defecate. You don't want him to learn that lesson! Hold your breath, step your dog away from the mess and finish the exercise before cleaning up.

3. Give it time. Like submissive urination, nervous defecation usually resolves itself over time. Meanwhile, try to be philosophical and remember that the dog isn't doing this behavior to punish you. He's doing it because he's scared.

FEAR-BITING

This section gives you advice on how to solve the problem presented by a fear-biter. However, the safety of your family has to come first. A fear-biter doesn't belong in a home with children. No matter how much you love the dog and want to save him, some situations just aren't going to work.

Fear-biters and children don't mix. Even a small dog can hurt a child, leaving the child with a lifelong fear of dogs. A larger dog can seriously injure a child. Since the dog's behavior isn't predictable—especially from a child's viewpoint—it isn't fair to the children in a household to keep the dog. It may be traumatic to find a new home for the dog—or, even worse, have him euthanized—but as horrible as that may be, it would be far worse to see your child's face ripped apart by a dog who unpredictably became startled by your child's play.

In addition, the quick, noisy movements of children are among the worst triggers for a fearful dog. Trying to help your dog overcome his propensity to fear-bite is prohibitively difficult in a household with small children. Don't even try to do it.

Dogs bite for many reasons, and not all biting behavior is fear-biting. Some dogs are aggressive and will assault people or animals who trespass on their properties. Many dogs will take on any other dog they meet to

A fear-biter believes he is cornered and must fight his way out.

determine who's the alpha dog. Still other dogs have been teased by children or adults and have decided that the best defense is a good offense, such as a growl or a bite to ward off the expected human behavior. All of these examples are problems that require the help of a capable dog trainer or behaviorist. However, none of them is necessarily fear-biting. In fact, compared to true fear-biting, the behaviors mentioned here are comparatively easy to remedy.

A fear-biter believes he's cornered and must fight his way out. The dog is frightened beyond his level of control and is acting entirely on instinct when he attacks. He literally cannot hear or respond to the voice of his owner.

The trigger to the dog's fear may or may not be something his owner can identify. Because the response is instinctive—and usually extremely swift—there may be no warning that a bite is coming. Moreover, the dog's perception of what is to be feared may not be very rational. Thus, the dog can lash out with a vicious bite in a situation in which a bite seems completely unprovoked and unpredictable.

Fear-biting isn't a behavior that's limited to dogs who appear to be obviously insecure. Fear-biting also occurs in dogs who seem normal to their owners until the dog is placed in a high-stress environment. The loving family Golden Retriever may inexplicably bite a child when the dog leaves his yard for the first time in months to attend the annual extended family reunion picnic. The gentle Doberman Pinscher who welcomes the mail carrier may decide to take the hand off the veterinarian rather than have his mouth inspected.

Fear-biting can be overcome, though. If you have a household that's tranquil and predictable, and if you feel you have a good relationship with the rational part of your dog, you may want to try tackling your dog's fear-biting tendencies. It's a long, difficult road, but if you love your dog and want to save his life, it can be very much worth the effort.

Try following these tips.

How to Stop Fear Biting

1. Train. Fear-biting will subside as your dog gains confidence. Your goal is to teach the dog to overcome his natural instincts in favor of learned behavior. After your dog is well-trained, he's able to suppress instinct in favor of the learned behavior when a situation presents itself that makes him feel the instinct to bite. When a fear-biter is in a situation that's likely to make him panic, have him perform a training exercise before he loses control. This keeps his brain on something he can deal with and pushes back the fear instinct.

2. Muzzle him. A muzzle is an indispensable tool as you're working through your dog's fear-biting. Your fear-biter should wear a muzzle in every situation in which he might respond by biting.

This means that the dog wears a muzzle to training class. It means that he wears a muzzle to the veterinarian's office. It means that he wears a muzzle when you walk him in the park. Of course, people will look at you oddly. Of course, they'll skirt around your dog and stare at him. It may embarrass you a little, but it will embarrass you a whole lot more if you give your dog the chance to bite someone.

The right muzzle is sturdy, gives your dog the opportunity to breathe through his mouth and to pant, and doesn't allow your dog to wiggle out of it. Wire muzzles used for racing Greyhounds are ideal. There are other quality muzzles available. Look for one at a local pet supply store, or order one through your veterinarian.

Before taking your dog out in a muzzle, get him used to wearing it in places in which he's comfortable. Let him wear it around the house for a few minutes three or four times a day. Praise him when you put the muzzle on him. Give him a treat. For a fear-biter, getting used to a muzzle is a routine that is as necessary as learning to accept a collar and leash.

Remember, the muzzle isn't punishment for your dog. It's a device designed to keep your dog from hurting you or someone else as you work through the dog's fear-biting behavior.

Although a muzzle can be an indispensable tool, don't think it's infallible. Dogs can sometimes wiggle their way out of muzzles, or muzzles can break. Give your dog enough room to allow others to be safe if the muzzle somehow comes off.

3. Expose your dog. Over time, your dog will need to be exposed to a variety of new situations. As with all fear behavior, the answer to the problem isn't to keep the dog locked away from real life. If the dog isn't exposed to the real world, over time he'll become more insecure in his own world and will become a danger even in his own yard and home.

Common sense—and the threat of possible lawsuits—tells you it's grossly wrong to expose other people to the danger of a dog bite while you're desensitizing your fear-biter. Keep him on a short leash. Don't let anyone pet or touch your dog.

Don't drag a dog into a busy mall parking lot if he's used to a quiet neighborhood backyard. Start him out slowly and work up. With his muzzle on, get to know your dog and the kind of stimulation that triggers his fear response. Then gradually expose him to that stimulation and help him learn to accept it.

4. Don't ignore his behavior. Unlike other fear behaviors, you can't just ignore your dog's fear-biting. When your dog begins fear-aggressive behavior, such as growling, give him a firm pop on the collar and tell him "no." Then redirect his attention by performing some simple training exercises. The training exercises are not punishment for his behavior. The exercises are to remind him that you're in control and that he should trust you to lead him safely.

When you correct your dog, don't yell at him, hit him or otherwise make a scene. Such abuse will just add to his anxiety and make him more likely to react with biting behavior. Just give him a quick pop on the collar or shake on the muzzle. Make the correction at the first sign of growling or snapping; don't wait until the dog is in an aggressive frenzy. If the dog is lunging and panicking, it's too late for the correction.

5. Praise him. Remember to praise your dog when he's behaving well in stressful situations. As he's coping quietly in a situation that would previously have caused him to snarl, tell him how proud your are of his good behavior. Give him a treat. Make a pleasant walk a happy experience for him.

6. Gradually remove the muzzle. When your dog has begun to behave very placidly with his muzzle on, begin to take him to controlled situations with the muzzle off. A good first place to remove the muzzle is in training class. Work with your trainer to decide when to take the muzzle off. When your dog has developed the confidence to do all of his exercises in proximity to the other dogs and people in class without a fear response, you've accomplished something very important.

After your dog has overcome his fear response in class, you may know your dog well enough to feel confident walking him without a muzzle on a public street. If you do this, remember that it's your responsibility to keep an eye on your dog 100 percent of the time. You have no right to expose other people or animals to danger because you weren't paying attention to your dog's subtle warning signs that he was too stressed to handle the situation.

Don't let other people pet your dog unless you are completely confident that he won't bite. Even when you think you're positive of your dog's response, hold onto his collar when he's being petted so you can control his head. If you feel him tense up, get him out of the situation.

No dog—particularly a fear-biter—should have to endure more than one person at a time petting him. It's uncomfortable for a dog to be surrounded by a crowd of strangers. Even after you've trained and desensitized your dog, he can regress to fear-biting if he feels he's cornered.

If you're in doubt, always bring the muzzle. It's much better to be safe than sorry.

Your dog's fearful aggression is a primitive instinct. Don't risk the safety of your children by attempting to work with a fear-biter in a home with youngsters. You can never completely trust a fear-biter, and you need to be vigilant with him every moment he's in a situation that stretches his comfort level. However, in the right household—and with patience, training and the use of a muzzle—your dog can learn to behave in a socially acceptable manner. He can become a pet that you and the world can live with.

Tess: A Lifetime Commitment

Tess is an accomplished obedience dog, as well as an absolutely adorable canine.

Tess, a strawberry-blonde and white Bearded Collie, seems like a giant ball of merrily bouncing fur as she executes her advanced training exercises. She pounces on her dumbbell as she retrieves it. She clears hurdles with ease. For good measure, owner Wanda Packard directs Tess to jump over another dog, retrieve her dumbbell and jump over the dog again as Tess brings the dumbbell back. Tess complies with a wagging tail and another enormous leap.

Tess is an accomplished dog in the obedience ring. She has earned her AKC CDX title, which demonstrates among other things that she heels and comes off-leash; retrieves objects on flat surfaces and over hurdles; and can remain motionless on the ground in a group of other dogs for five minutes while her owner is out of the building.

Tess not only passed these difficult tests, but she excelled in them. During her obedience career, she earned the award for the highest-scoring obedience dog at a regional Bearded Collie specialty show and

earned a place on a team that represented Oregon in regional dog obedience competition.

Becoming Fearful

Despite all these accomplishments, it hasn't always been easy to raise,
train and live with Tess. "I got Tess when she was 8 weeks old," reports
Wanda. "She seemed perfectly normal, although she was never really an
outgoing puppy." Wanda made sure that Tess had socialization opportunities. For example, she took Tess on volkswalks—long, low-stress walks
with groups of people—from the time Tess was 3 months old.

At age 6 months, Tess began to change. She began to shy away from
people. When two teenage girls came up, gawking and gushing, to pet
the unusual dog, Tess responded with a growl. With that, Tess learned
that growling and snapping kept people away. Wanda has to keep
vigilant watch over Tess, since the dog's natural instinct might be to
lash out in fear. Tess can be friendly one moment and become fear-
aggressive the next. "When Tess becomes fearful of something, she
panics and reacts according to her instincts," says Wanda. "I can never
entirely trust her."

Perhaps the most embarrassing of the fear behavior, however, has
been Tess's habit of defecating in situations that make the dog nervous.
Wanda says wryly, "I'm a basically shy person. This has been very hard
for me. I guess one good lesson of living with Tess is that I've learned
how to live with humiliation. It's made me a better person."

Why did Tess become so fearful and so different than Wanda's other
two outgoing, well-adjusted dogs? Wanda shakes her head with frustration. "I keep trying to figure out why she's so fearful. Sometimes I think
it was caused by some health problems and surgery she had when she
was young, but other dogs go through much worse experiences and
aren't afraid. Sometimes I wonder if someone teased her one day when
I wasn't there. I've wondered if her eyesight is okay. There's never an
answer, just asking myself over and over, 'Why, why, why?'"

No Regrets

Wanda also points out that nervous temperaments are not uncommon
among herding breeds. She theorizes that it's a fine line between shyness
and the suspiciousness that herding dogs must have toward anything
that might harm their flock.

The importance of training fearful dogs, Wanda underlines, cannot be overstated. She cautions owners of fearful puppies not to wait. The fact that a puppy is nervous about leaving the house makes it more important to go to school. For Tess, serious training was vital to her stability. Wanda believes training should be no-nonsense, but still positive and gentle. Frequent praise and much repetition are needed to encourage shy dogs.

Would Wanda do it over again? "I love Tess and would never give her up. However, I would warn people that a shy dog is a lifetime commitment. If something should happen to me, my other dogs could adjust to new owners. Tess couldn't. It's a big commitment having a fearful dog."

Then Wanda smiles. "What other people don't see, though, is what a great dog Tess is in her home environment, where she feels secure. She's so funny and smart. She makes up games, with their own rules, and teaches me how to play them. Because I'm the only one she truly loves, there's a special bond and a special relationship that we have. Tess is the most loving pet I've ever had. She's so tuned into me that she reads me like a neon light."

Tess sits quietly at Wanda's heel, her eyes gazing up adoringly. Wanda casually strokes Tess's unruly mop of hair. "Everything is a big deal to Tess, so it's easy to feel sorry for her sometimes," she says. "But when she accomplishes something, it means so much more. When she does well, she knows it." Wanda smiles and throws Tess's dumbbell, and Tess bounces joyfully over another dog to execute her retrieve.

Chapter Nine

Adding a Second Dog

Your new dog will teach your shy dog to have fun.

After you've had your fearful dog long enough to establish a close relationship with her, you might consider getting a second dog.

No, I'm not kidding.

I know that one dog seems like more than enough. But the right second dog can do things for your fearful dog that no human can ever do.

A second dog is often particularly useful to dogs who have been kenneled in the past. As one highly successful dog trainer and breeder explained it to me, "There are 'people' dogs and 'dog' dogs. If your fearful dog lived in a kennel, she's accustomed to other dogs. Living with another dog gives her a better sense of security."

An outgoing, friendly dog has a joy for living, a curiosity about her environment and an interest in people that a shy dog doesn't have. The right second dog can teach your first dog some of those traits.

For instance, many owners of shy dogs complain that their dogs are "too good." A shy dog may be so fearful of making a mistake that she won't do anything at all. The outgoing second dog will show the first dog how to play and how to take risks. Dogs can learn from watching other dogs, and the shy dog will learn the positive side of getting attention from strange humans. She'll find out that new places are exciting worlds to explore, not something to be dreaded. She'll learn that she can be a little bit assertive and the world won't end. She'll also discover that she can get in a little bit of trouble and life goes on just fine.

Dogs are often used as therapy dogs for people, providing companionship and unconditional love to people who are in nursing homes, hospices or similar settings. Think of a second dog as being a therapy dog for your fearful dog!

However, just as not every dog is cut out to be a therapy dog in a nursing home, not every one will make a good companion to your fearful dog. Look for these traits in selecting a second dog:

- **Boldness.** The new dog must be bold, happy and well-adjusted. Bringing in a nervous second dog will only compound your original problem: They'll teach each other their phobias and conditioned fear responses. Together, they'll think of things to be afraid of that neither one would think up by herself.

  You can imagine their doggie conversation: "Thanks for letting me know that vacuums are deadly, Fido. I wouldn't have guessed that. By the way, did you know the garbage can in the backyard is a known killer?" "No kidding, Princess. I'll watch out for it. By the way, steer clear of the south side of the fence. I think it's closing in on us!"

  Just as a shy dog can pick up positive responses to new situations from a bold dog, she can pick up fearful reactions from another shy dog.

- **No aggression.** The new dog should be friendly and bold, but must not be aggressive. An aggressive dog will terrorize your shy dog and will cause her to regress.

- **Similar size.** The new dog should be about the same size as your shy dog. Getting a dog who's much bigger than the first can be overwhelming to the first dog, and a bigger dog may not make an appropriate playmate. Likewise, a much smaller dog doesn't provide the same experience for your first dog as one that's close in size. Moreover, often a dog will accept another dog of her own breed (or general appearance) more easily than she'll accept a dog of a different breed.

- **Opposite sex.** Dogs of the opposite sex usually make the best friends with the least conflict. Although this is a good guideline, the personality of the two dogs is more important than their genders.

- **Youthfulness.** It's generally easier to introduce a puppy to your current dog than to introduce an older dog because the shy dog is less likely to be afraid of a puppy than of a mature dog. Again, an older dog with a great temperament can make a perfectly wonderful second dog, but it's usually less intimidating for a shy dog to learn to relate to a puppy.

If you've decided that a second dog is for you, and if you've found one you want to bring into your home, try these techniques to make the transition a smooth and happy one.

HOW TO BUILD A HEALTHY RELATIONSHIP

1. Introduce them on neutral territory. If possible, introduce your shy dog to the prospective new dog in a place neither considers to be her "territory."

Does your current dog seem to like the new dog? The worst indicator of a problem is absolute disinterest. A few growls from your current dog establishing dominance is actually a very positive sign. (Don't stop your shy dog from asserting her dominance with growls as long as she doesn't harm or unduly intimidate the other dog.)

2. Introduce them outside. Whether or not your first dog has previously met the second dog, make sure you don't bring the new dog directly into the house when you bring her home. You might, for example, leave the new dog in the car, get the second dog out of the house, take them both on a walk and then bring both dogs into the house together.

Present the second dog to the first dog. A highly respected breeder told me to tell my first dog, "This is your puppy. I got him for you, and he's yours to take care of." That breeder told me about a first dog who became such a doting surrogate mom to the puppy that she actually produced milk!

3. Pay attention to your first dog. For the first 10 days, pay 75 percent of the attention to your first dog and only 25 percent of your attention to the second dog. This is very hard to do, especially when the second dog is a puppy. Remind yourself that the second dog isn't used to being the center of all your attention—and your first dog is. If you follow this formula, after about 10 days, you'll see your first dog visibly relax. She'll be reassured that she's first in your loyalty and will accept the other dog. At that time, you can start giving both dogs equal time.

Some dogs, despite their shyness, are very territorial about their homes. Make sure that the first dog doesn't try to attack the new dog. Keep them separated for a while, if necessary. Correct aggressive behavior if it's a danger to the new dog. However, don't forget to be reassuring and loving to the first dog, and remember that the first dog gets 75 percent of the positive attention in the household.

4. Provide reassurance. Reassure your first dog that she's No. 1 in the pack. It's extraordinarily important that your shy dog isn't displaced by the bold, friendly new dog. Declare to both dogs that your first dog has seniority rights. Seniority is important to union members, senators and dogs. Greet your senior dog first when you come home at night. Feed the senior dog first. Practice her training exercises first. It isn't that you love one dog more than another; it's just that you recognize the seniority of your first dog. Enforce that behavior with the new dog so that she must defer to the senior dog. Don't allow the new dog to push the senior dog aside from what's rightfully hers.

Watch for subtle problems. After I'd had my second dog, Radar, for a couple of months, my shy dog's training routine suddenly fell apart. Goldie wouldn't do anything I'd ask of her, when previously she'd been very happy to do whatever I asked. She seemed mad at me. The trainer I was going to at the time said that Goldie was jealous of the new dog. I replied that I was following everything I was supposed to do. He shook his head and said, "You're doing something wrong. You watch the look on her face when you're with your new dog, and figure out what has her so upset."

I finally saw it. When Goldie was sitting next to me on the couch, the new dog would leap over her, balance on my shoulder and climb on top of my head. Since it's awfully hard to ignore a dog on your head, Goldie was forgotten for the moment. I looked at her face the next time it happened and saw the hurt in her eyes. I learned to disengage Radar without interrupting Goldie's attention. I looked for other times when Radar would attempt to steal my attention from Goldie and learned not to let it happen. As soon as I did so, Goldie's training routine began to spring back to its old ways. Much more importantly, she and Radar became best friends.

5. Schedule time with each dog. Spend individual time with each dog every day. If you don't, your dogs may bond so tightly with each other that you're left out of the equation.

6. Be prepared to return. Be prepared to give the second dog back to the breeder (or find a suitable home for her, if she's from an animal shelter) if the relationship between the dogs doesn't work out. Remember that your first loyalty has to be to your first dog. She has developed the fragile bond of trust with you that she may never be able to establish again if you break it now. You got the second dog for her as a therapy dog. If the second dog creates insurmountable problems for your first dog, you can't keep the second dog

The good news is that if you select an easy-going, friendly dog and carefully introduce her to your home, the odds of success are very high. If it doesn't work out, that friendly, easy-going dog will also adjust to a new home quickly. Be honest and straightforward with the person from whom you get the second dog about the importance of the second dog fitting into the home. Most breeders or shelters will be thrilled to place a dog with someone who is so loyal and caring toward the existing household pet.

Is it worth all this effort? It can be. Watching a happy, well-adjusted dog bring out the sense of fun and play in a shy dog is extraordinary to behold. A smart second dog will instinctively know how to teach your fearful dog. The new dog will show the shy dog that she can get in a little trouble and the world won't fall down on her head. The outgoing one will show the timid dog that the world is full of sights, sounds and smells that are to be savored rather than feared. The two of them will exercise muscles and instincts in ways that humans can't replicate. Your new dog will teach your shy dog to have fun.

Before I got my second dog, Goldie would tremble when we went somewhere in the car and she was expected to get out and face someplace new. Now she bounds out of the car with joyful enthusiasm. She has a curiosity that she never had before.

Because of my second dog, Goldie has learned to think and play. The day before writing this chapter, Radar was chewing on a toy that Goldie decided she wanted, but Radar wasn't about to give up. Goldie sat and watched him for a couple of minutes. Suddenly, her tail began to gently wag, and she got a dog smile on her face. She trotted into another room and brought back one of Radar's favorite squeaky toys. She brought it to me and dropped it at my feet to throw, all the time slowly wagging her tail. I knew something was up, so I watched her closely. I threw the squeaky toy. Radar looked up and streaked after the squeaky toy. Goldie, tail still slowly wagging, demurely walked over to the chew toy that had been in Radar's possession and happily took his place. It was having a second dog that taught Goldie how to think like a clever dog.

Of course, don't consider a second dog unless you're willing to give the time, effort and money that it takes to make a good home for her. There's no sin in deciding one dog is enough for you. With all the time and effort you've given to the first dog, you don't have to feel guilty about that decision.

The new dog also has needs of her own you'll have to meet. She may be No. 2 in the hierarchy, but she deserves the same amount of love and attention as the first dog. She also needs to be trained and to have time alone with just you. In return, you get all the love and affection she has to give.

The bond among you, your first dog and your second dog can be geometrically stronger than the bond between one person and one dog. You'll also witness the relationship between the two dogs, which will add enjoyment and amusement to your life.

After my experiences with a second dog, I can't imagine living with just one dog again. It's less than half the fun, for the dogs *and* the humans. I was able to bring Goldie a long way toward normalcy without a second dog. However, it was Radar who brought a relish of life to my once fearful, introverted first dog. Both dogs have brought their own brand of joy and love to me.

If a second dog in your home isn't a good choice for you right now, consider finding a regular playmate for your shy dog. If the playmate has the friendly, outgoing temperament to help your shy dog, a regular play date between the two of them will measurably help your nervous dog.

ADDING A FEARFUL DOG TO A HOME WITH EXISTING DOGS

Adding a fearful dog to your current dog household can be very successful. As in the case of adding any new dog, make sure the original dogs get to keep their seniority rights and place in the pack hierarchy.

Many people I spoke with described existing dogs in the household taking charge and helping out with the shy one. Other dogs can speed the recovery process for the shy dog by demonstrating healthy dog behavior. One person who introduced a shy dog into a home with three other dogs said, "The other dogs showed my new dog that she had to compete a little bit for attention. That was a good thing. It taught her to be more assertive. Of course, they also taught her to chew my shoes."

Watch carefully to make sure that the other dog or dogs in the family don't pick on the shy newcomer. Make sure the shy dog gets her share of victories in doggie games. One owner of a shy dog admitted, "When the dogs are playing fetch with me, I make sure I toss the toy very close to my shy dog every once in a while. Otherwise, the other two dogs always beat him to it because he's not aggressive enough to really go for it. He doesn't know he's getting special help. He's just proud he got the toy."

There's a lot of joy in a multiple-dog household because dogs enjoy living with other dogs. Adding a new, shy dog to a household with one or more other dogs can be a rewarding experience for both the owner and the dogs.

Briggs: A Throw-Away Dog

⅋

Briggs and owner Claudia (right) earned a coveted Highest Scoring Dog in Trial award under difficult conditions.

A shadow of sadness passes over Claudia Van Gee's eyes as she describes the first time she saw Briggs, her rescued Shetland Sheepdog. "He was 6 months old," she says, "and he'd obviously had a bad time of it. He was very timid and just didn't know how to deal with people. He'd cringe if you moved your arm suddenly, as if he'd been hit." Still, Claudia sensed a great spirit in the fearful young dog. "He was just the most beautiful Sheltie pup I'd ever seen," she says with a smile. She had no trouble deciding to bring the pup home to join her family of dogs.

An Easy Dog to Train

Claudia believes that Briggs was abused before he came to her. "He didn't know how to do any of the things that dogs do," she explains. "He wasn't housebroken. He didn't play with toys. He seemed so afraid of doing something wrong that he just didn't do anything."

Right away, Claudia's other dogs began to help socialize Briggs. "The other dogs taught Briggs. They showed him the home routine of house training, protecting the house, interacting with people and other dogs, and playing with toys." Claudia adds with a laugh, "They even taught him to get up on the bed."

Claudia, a veteran obedience trial competitor, enrolled Briggs in obedience class at the first opportunity. He wasn't an easy dog to train. She remembers the first time they attempted a "come" command off-leash. Briggs was sitting across the room and was supposed to trot smartly to Claudia when she called him. Instead, the dog panicked and ran for cover under some benches.

After his inauspicious start, Briggs has come a long way. He has received his AKC Canine Good Citizen certificate. He has passed his therapy dog certification. Most impressively, Briggs has earned his C.D.X. (Companion Dog Excellent) title from the American Kennel Club and the United Kennel Club. To earn a C.D.X., a dog must (among other things) heel off-leash; come when called, then lie down instantly at the verbal or signal cue, then get up and come to the handler when called again; retrieve a dumbbell over a high jump; and remain in a three-minute sit and five-minute down without moving in a group of other dogs while the handler is out of the room.

Going for the Gold

The high point of Briggs's obedience work to date was to win Highest Scoring Dog in Trial and Highest Aggregate Scoring Novice Dog at the British Columbia Shetland Sheepdog Club competition. "The weather was ice cold," recalls Claudia. "The competition included four trials over two days, which is tiring for the dogs and the handlers. Briggs did his best performance on the second day of the trial. That day, he showed what heart is in an animal."

Claudia says taking fearful dogs to training class is imperative if they are to overcome their behavior problems. "Classes bring more situations to the dog than the average pet owner encounters," she explains. "The dog learns that his owner won't let any of those strange new situations hurt the dog. The dog learns to trust his owner." Claudia adds with a grin, "Besides, they learn there's food involved with this obedience stuff. They learn to love class!"

Claudia emphasizes that training a fearful dog isn't the easiest path to follow. "Timid dogs aren't for someone who wants to be the hottest trainer in town," she warns. "They usually learn more slowly than bolder dogs. Briggs still shuts down whenever he learns something new, and it's like dealing with his problems all over again. But he trusts me, so he'll try. I just have to whisper to him, 'You're an awfully good dog, and I love you.' It's so exciting to watch the light go on when he figures out what's expected of him. It makes it all worth it."

Putting the Past Behind Him

Some traces of Briggs's past will always be with him. He's still afraid of men who smoke; Claudia assumes that Briggs's abuser was a cigarette smoker. To this day, Briggs doesn't enjoy petting the same way Claudia's other dogs do. Happily, though, the shadow of Brigg's puppyhood is mostly behind him. Claudia says that when Briggs was 3 years old, everything just clicked, and he relaxed noticeably. Today, he's a happy, energetic dog who loves to play with children. He has a regular routine of watching through the sliding glass door, waiting for a squirrel who visits the deck. When the squirrel shows up, Briggs barks with obvious relish from inside the house while the squirrel calmly eats beyond his reach.

What advice does Claudia have for someone considering adopting a timid dog? "Do it. Don't be intimidated by what other people may tell you." She cautions, however, "Look at your lifestyle, and be sure you have the time to give to your dog. These dogs need extra time with you. But the time you spend will be worth it. You won't believe how closely you will bond to your dog. Over the years, you'll develop a trust between you that you may never feel with a 'normal,' outgoing dog."

Claudia pauses reflectively before she adds, "You have to work with the dog God gave you. Some dogs are happy and outgoing, but some dogs are shy or really not all that intelligent. In a throw-away society, it's nice to keep a dog with limitations. They can excel and go beyond your imagination."

Chapter Ten

Fun, Games and Activities

Dogs can teach humans to fetch even faster than humans can
teach dogs to fetch.

You've done the hard part: Your dog is trained. You've socialized him and he has put the worst of his fears behind. It's time to have some fun with your dog!

LEARNING TO PLAY

Fearful dogs often don't know how to play. Whether the hesitancy to play comes from neglect (it's hard to play when you're living in a crate 24 hours a day) or just a plain inability to relax, you may have to teach your fearful dog how to play.

This chapter will give you some ideas for spontaneous as well as organized fun and games that both you and your dog will enjoy. *Warning:* Once your dog learns how to play, he might become addicted! You'll be enticed to play games with him when you might otherwise be watching television, doing crossword puzzles or writing one more version of a report that's due at the office. Well, maybe both of you can benefit from a little more play!

Fetch

Fetch is great fun for both you and your dog. It's also one of the most emotionally and physically healthy games your dog can play. Although there's an occasional dog who never learns to play fetch, most master the game easily and quickly. Dogs also almost never tire of playing fetch.

Dogs who have lived in kennels or been kept in crates for hours on end are often uncoordinated. Playing fetch is one of the fastest ways to help improve your dog's coordination.

Try this game someplace where your dog feels the safest—you might want to start out in your living room.

Most dogs will naturally chase a toy and bring it back to you. Show your dog the toy. Wave it around. Put it close to his nose and quickly move it away. In an excited voice, ask the dog if he really wants it. Then roll the toy across the floor. Most dogs at that point will chase the toy and pick it up. After he learns to pick the toy up when it's rolling, start throwing the toy through the air for him.

If your dog is interested in the toy but vague about the concept of retrieving, chase the toy yourself and bring it back. (Dogs can teach humans to fetch even faster than humans can teach dogs to fetch.)

Make sure your dog brings the toy back to you when he fetches. If you keep calling him over to you when he's got the toy, he'll soon figure out that he's got to bring you the toy for the game to continue.

When your dog picks up the toy, give him a consistent, encouraging phrase such as "Bring it here." When I want to play fetch with Goldie, I just say, "Bring it here," and she finds a favorite toy to bring me for a rousing game of fetch.

Periodically, try to play fetching games someplace your dog finds less comfortable. Progress from the living room to the backyard. Go from the backyard to the neighborhood park. Fenced tennis courts make a great place to play. Graduate from the neighborhood park to a park you haven't explored yet. As your dog becomes relaxed enough to play his favorite game in these varied situations, his fears will melt away.

There are endless variations to the game. One variation is "catch," in which the dog is supposed to catch the object in midair. To teach catch, gently toss a favorite tidbit or small, soft toy directly at your dog's face. If he doesn't catch it in midair, grab it off the ground before he can get it. Repeat the process until your dog has learned to snatch the tidbit or toy out of the air. It won't take long for him to figure out the game and enjoy it.

Frisbee is also a fun form of fetch. Get a dog Frisbee and have a great time in the backyard or your local park.

Tug-of-War

Most dog-training books sternly advise people never to play tug of war with their dogs because it heightens aggression and encourages a dominant dog to challenge his owner. One of the guilty pleasures of owning a very submissive dog is the opportunity to play this game together. If your dog is always submissive and never aggressive (no fear-biters should be playing this game), go ahead and have some fun. Your dog will pick the soft toy he likes to tug on. Make sure not to overwhelm your dog with overly rough play.

Let your dog win occasionally—he'll feel like hot stuff!

Speak (and Other Naturally Occurring Behaviors)

Nervous dogs are sometimes barkers. One way to control barking is to teach it on command. When your dog barks, say, "Speak." Then tell him he's brilliant. When he learns to associate the barking with the word "speak," he should bark when you tell him to and be less likely to bark at other times.

When your dog is barking on command, you can start doing a hand signal (such as wiggling your finger). Over time, he'll bark when you wiggle your finger. Then you can play games with it. Ask him the square root of 16, and wiggle your finger until he barks four times. As long as you can keep your math straight, your friends will be really impressed with your dog!

You can teach your dog to associate any naturally occurring behavior with any word. My little Papillons love to bounce up and down. I've taught them to do it on cue when I say "popcorn," so now they do a food imitation!

Goldie naturally positioned herself into a "beg" posture when she reached for a treat. I associated that posture with the word "please." Now I ask Goldie to "say please," and she puts herself into the "beg" position for her reward.

Keep It Fun

You can teach your dog endless tricks by saying a word when he performs an action. He'll learn to associate the word with the action—and the fact that he gets plenty of praise.

Remember, this is fun. It's a game. Your dog is already working hard all the time. He's going to class and enduring new places. Some of your time together needs to be the delicious joy of playing games together. So play fetch, tug-of-war, speak and a dozen other games. Laugh with each other when you do.

Let Your Dog Be Wild and Crazy

Every once in a while, a dog needs to be a dog. Let him chase squirrels or birds (in a fenced-in enclosure). Give him opportunities to play with non-aggressive dogs his own size, racing around the yard until they're exhausted. Every dog, even the smallest Chihuahua or a snubnosed Pekingese, has a little bit of a wild creature lurking under the skin. Let him get in touch with the predator inside—it'll add to his confidence. Both of you will enjoy the thrill of his running, chasing and circling. Laugh together when he's run himself ragged.

After all, laughter really is the best medicine.

AGILITY TRAINING: CONFIDENCE-BUILDING FUN

The action, exercise and sheer fun of agility can act as therapy for your shy dog. Check out a class to see if the activity is for you.

It's a joy to watch dogs run an agility course. They leap over hurdles; run through large, tunnel-like tubes; dance across catwalks much like 5-feet-high balance beams; and scramble up and down wooden A-frames. In order to qualify for titles, the dogs have to complete the exercises at basically a dead run.

The look of happiness on a dog's face as he runs the course is undeniable. Many of the dogs bark enthusiastically as they successfully negotiate a jump. Tails wag. Perhaps no other organized dog sport can match the entertainment of agility. It's also a great way to help a shy dog overcome his inhibitions.

Your dog trainer can probably direct you to a good class or can help you locate an agility competition where you can meet people who teach classes.

If you and your dog meet the following criteria, it's worth finding a good class and seeing if the sport is for you:

1. Good training. Your dog must be relatively well-trained. (You knew those training classes were worthwhile!) Agility is done off-leash, so your dog has to be trained well enough not to head out of the building when you take off his leash.

2. Healthy dog. Your dog must be healthy and fit. The goal of agility is for your dog to run an obstacle course, so he needs to be healthy enough to jump, climb and run. He can't be overweight (since that puts major stress on his body at the end of a jump) or have a debilitating condition such as hip dysplasia. Although the sport is fun

The action, exercise and sheer fun of agility can act as
therapy for your shy dog.

and appropriate for most dogs, some long-bodied dogs (such as
Dachshunds) and large-bodied dogs (such as Mastiffs) should get a
veterinarian's approval before participating in agility.

3. Reasonably healthy human. You also must be reasonably
healthy. You don't need to be as fit as your dog, since he'll be doing all
the jumping, tunneling and climbing. On the other hand, you'll have
to keep up with him while he's doing these things, so this isn't a good
activity for a person with mobility problems. If you ever compete in an
agility trial, you'll see that it's definitely an advantage for the handler
to be quite fit in order for the dog to post the fast times necessary to
qualify for titles.

4. Readiness. You must be ready to experience an extraordinary
bond with your dog. The handler and dog are a team. Working
together with your dog in agility is one of the strongest, fastest ways to
cement a great bond with your dog.

Beginners' Class

A beginning-level agility class will teach your dog how to jump safely.
You'll start out with one jump and work up to a series of jumps. You'll

begin to work on the other apparatus at low heights and add to the height over time.

Advanced class will develop your technique further, and you'll learn to work much faster. You'll work a whole course rather than a few jumps at a time. You'll learn to work in partnership with your dog as you navigate changing courses in varying conditions.

Look for a class where beginners and dogs with temperament problems are welcome. Shy dogs don't make the best competitive agility dogs, since competitive agility rewards bold dogs who run fast and jump high in strange, noisy surroundings. If the agility trainer's only goal is winning competitions, your dog may not fit in.

Find an agility trainer who's interested in helping your dog overcome his fears. When a shy dog realizes he can leap over high jumps, vault through hoops and climb tall objects, his confidence will soar.

Agility can bring out your dog's athleticism and boost his confidence—and it will surely increase the bond between the two of you. Give it a try!

ORGANIZED DOG SPORTS

After all the time and effort you've put into your dog, you've been rewarded with a fabulous pet. You and your terrific dog might want to check out some organized dog activities together. As your dog recovers from his fear, it's very satisfying to go places and do things together. It's also great fun to show off your dog's abilities. Here's a summary of the activities that Briggs, Colter, Goldie, Tarah and Weazie (the dogs profiled in this book) have undertaken. Try some of them with your dog—you'll both have a good time!

AKC Canine Good Citizen Test

To pass this test, the dog is given a series of challenges, such as demonstrating he'll walk on a loose lead with his owner, walking through a small crowd of people, sitting while a person handles him, remaining calm while someone makes distracting noises such as clanging pans and sitting quietly by the handler's side while the handler shakes hands with a person who also has a dog by his or her side.

These tests are frequently given at pet fairs, fun matches (practice dog shows) and in some training classes. Although the test is sponsored by the American Kennel Club (AKC), dogs don't have to be purebreds to participate. You must be able to demonstrate that your dog is licensed and has a current rabies vaccine (you're supposed to be a good citizen, too!).

Briggs, Colter, Goldie, Tarah and Weazie are all AKC Canine Good Citizens.

Obedience Competitions

You've taken your dog to a great training school, right? You've had to work longer and harder than your classmates in order for your dog to comfortably and reliably execute his exercises no matter what else is going on. Why not get an obedience title and show the world just how much your dog knows?

The AKC and the UKC both hold many obedience competitions throughout the country each year. Other, smaller organizations also hold competitions. Dogs competing for AKC titles must be purebred and either registered with the AKC or have an Indefinite Listing Privilege (ILP), which indicates that a dog is obviously purebred but doesn't have registration papers. Dogs with ILPs can't compete for the "beauty pageant" aspect of dog shows, but they can compete in obedience and other performance events.

If your dog isn't a purebred, don't despair. Your mixed-breed dog has the chance to win ribbons and titles through the United Kennel Club (UKC). The UKC deserves some sort of medal for giving the owners of mixed-breed dogs the chance to be involved in the great sport of obedience with their dogs.

Three levels of obedience competition exist: Novice, Open and Utility. Each requires progressively more skills.

Briggs, Challenge, Colter, Goldie, Tarah, Tess and Weazie have all earned obedience titles.

Agility Competitions

Agility competitions have become even more popular than obedience competitions. Colter and Weazie both earned agility titles—and had a great time competing.

Four major sponsoring organizations exist for agility events: the United States Dog Agility Association (USDAA), the North American Dog Agility Council (NADAC), the United Kennel Club (UKC) and the American Kennel Club (AKC). Mixed breeds are welcome at

Why not get an obedience title and show the world
just how much your dog knows?

USDAA, NADAC and UKC competitions; dogs must be purebred to
compete in AKC agility competitions.

Beginner, intermediate and advanced levels of competition exist
in each organization, but the organizing bodies have various titles and
differences in competition. No matter which organization sponsors the
event, though, the dogs always enjoy the running, jumping and climbing that define agility.

To earn titles, dogs must go through the course within a specified
time period. Successful dogs are both fast and responsive to their
handlers' directions.

Therapy Work

Briggs, Colter and Weazie provide service to people as certified therapy
dogs. Certified therapy dogs are welcome in nursing homes, hospitals,
hospices and other places where isolated or ill people can benefit from
the healing powers of dogs. Certifying organizations are Therapy Dog
International; Therapy Dogs, Inc.; and the Delta Society.

In order to receive certification, dogs must demonstrate that they are calm when petted by strangers, that they aren't upset by sudden noises, and that they deal well with people using walkers, wheelchairs, canes and other apparatus.

Working Certificate

Challenge earned a Working Certificate (W.C.). To earn this designation, a dog must demonstrate hunting instinct and bird-retrieving ability.

Herding Instinct Test

Colter passed a herding instinct test. To pass this test, a dog must show an innate ability to approach and herd a flock of sheep, ducks or cattle.

Lure Coursing

Sight hounds test their speed, agility and endurance chasing plastic bags (instead of rabbits or gazelles) in lure coursing competitions. Tarah is a Field Champion in lure coursing.

An Unlimited Range of Activities

Believe it or not, there are dozens of dog activities that the dogs profiled in this book haven't tried. More than ever before, there are countless organized activities you can enjoy with your dog. These include tracking events, drafting, water rescue, a variety of field trial events, weight pulling, earth dog events, herding competitions, fly ball, Frisbee and conformation competition, among other activities.

Whatever interests you, try it with your dog. The more you do with him, the better pet and partner he will be. Your dog will benefit from the experiences you give him, and you'll also have a great time, learn new things, go new places and meet new people. Your once-fearful dog can be the catalyst for new interests and activities for you. Enjoy the opportunities that are available to both of you!

Your Dog:
Another Success Story

The day isn't far away when someone will say, "I wish I had a dog just like yours!"

Throughout this book, you've read the stories of other fearful dogs. All of those dogs became a joy to their proud owners. Many of the dogs profiled in this book have accomplished a lot—some would fit anyone's definition of a "super dog." Each dog had substantial problems that the owners had to address. The stories of these dogs prove that fearfulness can happen in any breed and under any set of circumstances.

You don't have to be an experienced dog trainer to transform your dog. The owners of the dogs who were profiled in this book are as varied as the animals they love. Some were people well-recognized in the world of competitive dog shows. Two of the owners had never had a dog before their shy one. What the owners had in common was devotion to their dogs and the willingness to undertake the work to help their dogs transition into great pets.

Your dog can make the same dramatic progress that the dogs in this book achieved. It's up to you to make it happen.

Give your dog a hug, talk to him in an upbeat voice and get started! Believe in your dog's ability to transform. The day is not far away when someone will say, "I wish I had a dog just like yours!" The journey you and your dog are about to undertake is worth every step. You have a joyous adventure ahead of you.

Index